© 2015 Venture Publications Ltd

ISBN 978 1905 304 58 5

Front cover: Glasgow took two batches of double-decker bodies from NCB, 20 on AEC Regent chassis in 1948 and a further 20 on Daimler chassis in 1949. D19 of the latter batch is seen in service in the undertaking's distinctive livery. *(Courtesy STTS/Ian Dunnett, OnLine Transport Archive)*

Rear cover: Newcastle trolleybus 501 (LTN 501), with a Sunbeam S7 chassis, was delivered in September 1948. When it was withdrawn from service 17 years later it was presented to the City's Museum of Science and Engineering in view of its local interest. Subsequently it was completely restored by the Beamish Museum following which it was loaned to the Trolleybus Museum at Sandoft, for a number of years, where it is seen here. *(Ian Stubbs)*

Title page: Aberdeen Corporation NCB-bodied Daimler CWD6 bus, No.72 of 1947, is seen with a 1949 Pickering-bodied centre-entrance bogie tramcar (probably No. 26) at the Bridge of Dee terminus and turning circle. The tramcar is on the 'main-line' service (No.1) from the Bridge of Don and the bus is on a feeder service (No.13) from Garthdee. The handsome tramcar outshines the conservative styling of the NCB bus but the trams were abandoned in May 1958. Bus 72 soldiered on, however, until sale in October 1963. It is seen in its second livery with some strengthening to both front and rear bulkheads. *(Courtesy STTS/Ray DeGroute, OnLine Transport Archive)*

This London Transport Guy Arab with its Park Royal body was saved for posterity by John Lines. As they were built by using Park Royal components, the NCB bodies were almost identical. *(STA)*

The British Bus and Truck Heritage

Northern Coachbuilders

A history of the Company
and its products

by

Geoff Burrows and Bob Kell

Computer Origination and Design: John A Senior

Venture *publications*

PREFACE

I was very flattered to be asked to write this Preface. Then I realised that I was probably the youngest employee in 1943, and as I was 80 when I was approached, it left a rather limited choice.

It was quite a thrilling time for me, just having left school and waiting for call-up for the Navy, to have a wage, freedom and the feeling that I was doing something for the war effort in the meantime. As I had done machine drawing at school, I was put into the NCB drawing office on pretty primitive work.

The highlights of the time I was there were the 'socials' in the airship shed at Cramlington, incredibly vast, almost pitch black because of the blackout, no heating in the shed or in the bus that took us there and back; it certainly cooled one's ardour.

After de-mob in 1947 I claimed reinstatement and worked until the founder of the company, Sam Smith, died and that almost signed the death warrant for NCB because the punitive death duties had to be paid by the sale of most of his assets. A very sad situation for a proud producer of some wonderful work. The Authors have produced a fascinating work and the research is absolutely remarkable – a real eye-opener to me.

Peter Else.
Former Sales Director,
Ringtons Ltd.

These horse-drawn vans were designed and built by the craftsmen of Ringtons. They were used to deliver tea to householders in the north east where they became an established institution and a fine sight on the road. The livery, green and black with gold lettering and signwriting, was always immaculate. Seen in this picture are seven of them, standing outside the new Ringtons headquarters in Algernon Road in the east end of Newcastle in 1928. *(Courtesy Ringtons)*

CONTENTS

THE AUTHORS

Geoff Burrows

Geoff was born and raised in South Shields, and after leaving school became an apprentice draughtsman at NCB. When the firm closed, he went into the electrical engineering industry, working in design and later management. His duties took him around the United Kingdom, western Europe and north America. Because he retained his interest in transport, he always carried a camera. This led to one or two moments of embarrassment when he was discovered with one in areas of maximum security.

He has written numerous articles in several transport magazines, and is the author of The Trolleybuses of South Shields, published in 1974. He has been writing a 'Question and Answer' column in Classic Bus magazine since 1994.

Geoff has been married for nearly sixty years, and has two sons and a daughter, all married. There are also four grandchildren. None of them has the slightest interest in buses, but two are railway enthusiasts and one is an expert on trams, at home and abroad. After going from Tyneside to the Wirral, Geoff moved with his family to Hampshire, where he lives today.

'Ask Geoff'– from Classic Bus.

Most buses looked well in the complex livery of the City of Oxford fleet – but what a disfiguring advertisement! The early post-war standard body on the Oxford vehicle, not at its best in lowbridge form, nevertheless survives the mildly intrusive Clayton destination box and 'shoulder' under the drivers cab window to present a genteel and welcoming 'face' to the fortunate traveller. By comparison, opposite, vehicles made a dramatic impact in the deep yellow and cream adopted by Newcastle Transport in 1949 and which had already been used for trolleybuses. The elegant radiator of the post-war AEC Regent (and Regal) III enhanced most coachwork and the Bramham 8ft wide body was at its best on the Regent chassis. A clean, balanced and integrated design.

THE AUTHORS

Bob Kell

Bob Kell with DPT 848, a 1939 Tiger TS8 formerly with Sunderland District.

Bob grew up near to a main road out of Sunderland and was a frequent bus traveller with parents and grandparents from birth. He also travelled independently to school every day, changing buses, from the age of four. Travel to and from school every day was always more engaging than school itself, of which he remembers little.

This fascination has continued to a greater or lesser degree at times. Northern Coachbuilders was first encountered with travel on Sunderland District's wartime rebodied AEC Regent double-deckers and later Northern General's standardisation on the post-war NCB body for Guy and AEC double-deckers. The link with the monthly home deliveries of Rington's tea was not then apparent.

With the realisation that NCB had been the major coachbuilders between Leeds and Edinburgh, whose products were seen throughout the country in the 1940s/50s, he started a history of the firm in the 1980s with information from a group of ex-NCB employees who met regularly in Newcastle. Ringtons staff were also supportive. Contact with the professional photographer James Riddell before he retired gave access to his collection of mainly glass negatives with its record of all forms of road transport. Turners of Newcastle photographed post-war production and were also helpful in printing their collection. These collections are now in Newcastle City Library and Tyne & Wear Archives respectively and their staff time is also appreciated.

While working in higher education, vehicle preservation has been a continuing interest and riding on David Slater's excellent NCB-bodied Newcastle AEC Regent a particular pleasure. He is also Treasurer of the North East Bus Preservation Trust Ltd and has a number of other transport histories in preparation.

ACKNOWLEDGEMENTS

It would not have been possible to write this book without the help and contributions of many people. Peter Else, former Sales Director of Ringtons Ltd, encouraged and supported the project. Many former staff at Northern Coachbuilders Ltd have provided a great deal of information on their work including Jack Simmons, Ken Challinor, George Graham, Earl Gibson, Joe Irwin, Harry Nixon, Joe Rudd, Andy Nichol, Doug Pargeter and George Dobson.

Amongst the many to have provided information are Steven Morris and Alan Millar of Buses magazine, Gavin Booth of Classic Bus, Steve Stevens-Stratton of Vintage Roadscene, Chris Taylor, Hon Librarian and Registrar of the Historic Commercial Vehicle Society, Tom Robinson of the Sheffield Transport Study Group, The London Omnibus Traction Society, The Omnibus Society and the PSV Circle, and we gratefully acknowledge their contributions. Tony Wickens and Les Brunton of the Beamish Museum Tramway Group, and colleagues from the Birmingham and Midland Museum of Transport and the Trolleybus Museum at Sandtoft have all assisted with information.

The files of Bus & Coach, Buses Illustrated, Commercial Motor, Modern Transport, Motor Transport, Passenger Transport Journal, The Railway Gazette, Transport World, Trolleybus Magazine, Vintage Commercial Vehicle, Vintage Roadscene, The Northern Echo, The Newcastle Evening Chronicle and The Shields Gazette all revealed useful material. Many written records have been consulted, and we would particularly like to thank the staff of the Newcastle City Library, Newcastle University Library, South Tyneside Libraries & Museums, Mandy Watmough of Hampshire County Library, Durham County Records Office, The Imperial War Museum and Companies House. Countless books have also been studied to search for the many references and pictures of NCB and this Publisher's detailed histories of other coachbuilding concerns have also been most useful in many ways.

The formal photographic record of the products of Northern Coachbuilders was entrusted to two professional businesses. From 1934 to 1946 James Riddell of Chillingham Road, Newcastle was the photographer and the authors wish to thank Mr Riddell for his co-operation before his retirement, and Olive Graham of the Local Studies Centre of Newcastle City Library, where Mr Riddell's collection is cared for. From 1946, Turner's (Photography) Ltd of Pink Lane, Newcastle held the contract, and their staff were of great assistance until the collection was entrusted to the Tyne & Wear archives at Blandford House. Chief Archivist Elizabeth Rees and her staff have been most helpful, and have made available the Turner daybooks, which provide the dates of many of the photographs. The authors wish to thank most sincerely both Newcastle City Library and Tyne & Wear archives for their co-operation.

The list of enthusiasts who have helped is almost endless, amongst them are Phillip Battersby, Keith Beedon, John Bennet, Gerry Bixley, Stewart Brett, John Challinor, Allan Condie, Mike Dare, Bob Davis, Michael Dryhurst, Mike Eyre, Mike Fenton, Ian Findlay, Cyril Golding, Paul Gray, Bob Grey, Phillip Groves, Robin Hannay, David Harvey, John Hinchliffe, Tony Holdsworth, Roy Jetten, Phillip Kirk, John Lines, Alan Little, Geoff Lumb, Iain MacGregor, Peter McCutcheon, Robert McGilvray, Roy Marshall, Bruce Maund, Gordon Mills, Harry Postlethwaite, John Reynolds, John Shearman, David Slater, Ian Souter, Alan Townsin, David Wayman, John Whitehead and Jim Wilkinson, but we sincerely apologise to the many others whose names we have omitted, some of whom are sadly no longer with us.

We must particularly thank Gerry Bixley, who uncomplainingly adapted his work to accommodate the nit-picking requirements of the authors, and made an invaluable contribution to the book with his 4mm scale drawing of the standard NCB double-deck body. Our special thanks go to John Herdman, former Managing Director of Bus Bodies (SA) Ltd , who was the draughtsman responsible for the NCB trolleybus body production drawings during the early post-war years. He provided much information and photographs that would otherwise not have been available to the authors.

The photographs that appear between the covers of this book are acknowledged individually, those from Riddell and Turner's coming from the joint authors collections. Many more pictures were offered to the authors than could be used, and we sincerely thank all those who submitted them. We apologise to those whose pictures we have used without acknowledgement, though we have searched diligently for their provenance, and their anonymous contributions to this history are felt to be important enough to use.

Last, but be no means least, we must thank our wives Sylvia and Glynis for their tolerance when our homes have been filled with piles of seemingly useless photographs, paper and books, and their encouragement, particularly during the moments when the task appeared to be beyond hope of completion. John Senior of Venture Publications finally – and cheerfully – took on the seemingly impossible task of taking this mass of material and turning it into the splendid production you now see. We both owe him a debt of gratitude though he assures us he would not have wanted to miss the opportunity to add another notch to his list of bodybuilders' publications, particularly one with such a wealth of fine material.

Geoff Burrows & Bob Kell

September 2014

Travel to and from work for most of the workforce was either on foot or by public transport, and here we see the end of the working day as much-rebuilt 1901 Gateshead & District tram No. 44 waits to leave the short stretch of track at the Haymarket end of Claremont Road. This track had been left intact after the trams to Spital Tongues had been withdrawn in the 1930s, providing a useful terminus. The men boarding the tram are NCB employees, as also is the drawing office typist about to pass the tram on her bike. *(George Hearse)*

Newcastle's industrial background

Taking coal to Newcastle was once a common expression, indicating that it had plenty of its own and so did not need any to be brought in. Coal mining in the area had begun in Roman times and expanded rapidly in the 18th and 19th centuries as the improvement of roads enabled the coal to be sold further afield. Although not the birthplace of the Industrial Revolution, the area played a major role in what was to change the way we lived and worked. The need to move coal quickly and cheaply led to the birth of the railways. Initially, horses dragged wagons along plate-ways and then the invention of the locomotive allowed the Stockton and Darlington railway to open in 1825. Until recent years, coal was still king in the region. In 1900 there were 37,000 employed in the Northumberland coalfield and a further 100,000 in the neighbouring Durham coalfield.

This abundance of coal enabled many other manufacturing processes to start up in the area. The iron and steel industry developed which in turn supplied the heavy engineering works. The Tyne Bridge was built by Dorman Long of Middlesbrough and opened on October 10th 1928 by King George V. Four years later they built the bridge which crosses Sydney harbour, to a similar design. The move from wooden ships to those made from iron created the ship-building industry of Tyneside which was renowned for names such as Swan Hunter. Perhaps the most famous ship built on the Tyne was the 1906 Mauretania, it held the 'blue riband' for the fastest Atlantic crossing for 25 years. The shipyards supplied many of the naval vessels needed during the two world wars. Manufacture of armaments has a long history in the area and the works of Armstrong Whitworth, later to become Vickers Armstrong, also contributed greatly to the war effort.

Railway locomotives were built at the Stephenson works in Newcastle until 1901 when, due to lack of room for expansion, it moved to Darlington. The depression of the 1930s caused large-scale unemployment in the area, particularly in the heavy industries, 19 shipyards closed in 1930.

In 1936 the Team Valley Trading Estate, Gateshead was established to encourage the light industries in the region. It was recognition of the dangers of relying too heavily upon a small number of manufacturing industries

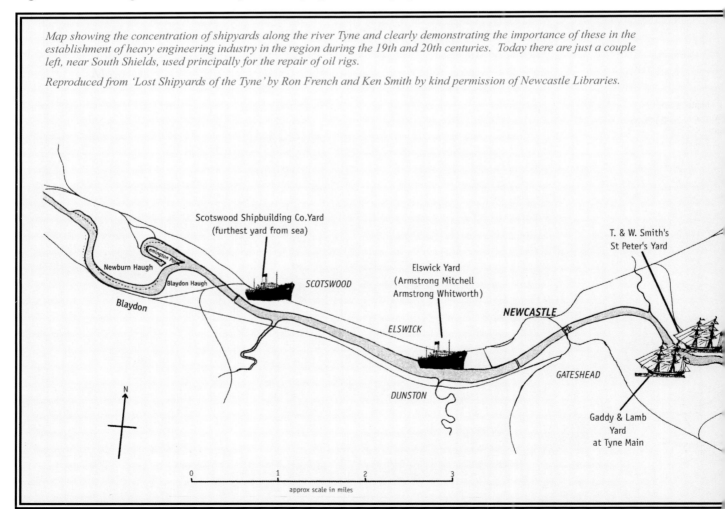

Map showing the concentration of shipyards along the river Tyne and clearly demonstrating the importance of these in the establishment of heavy engineering industry in the region during the 19th and 20th centuries. Today there are just a couple left, near South Shields, used principally for the repair of oil rigs.

Reproduced from 'Lost Shipyards of the Tyne' by Ron French and Ken Smith by kind permission of Newcastle Libraries.

which employ many people. The region had been designated a Special Area in the Special Areas Act of 1934.

Other industries which have existed, or still exist, in the area include the famous Newcastle Breweries, flour milling, confectionery, glass manufacture, pottery, soap and chemicals. Tyneside played a leading part in the development of electrical power and light, as it was in Gateshead that Sir Joseph Swan invented the incandescent electric lamp. Manufacture of electrical equipment then developed in the area.

Today's Newcastle sees the benefit of investment and improvement in railed transport, local and national, new businesses springing up, and an air of greater confidence in the future reflected in the wonderfully revitalised waterfront and elsewhere in and around the city.

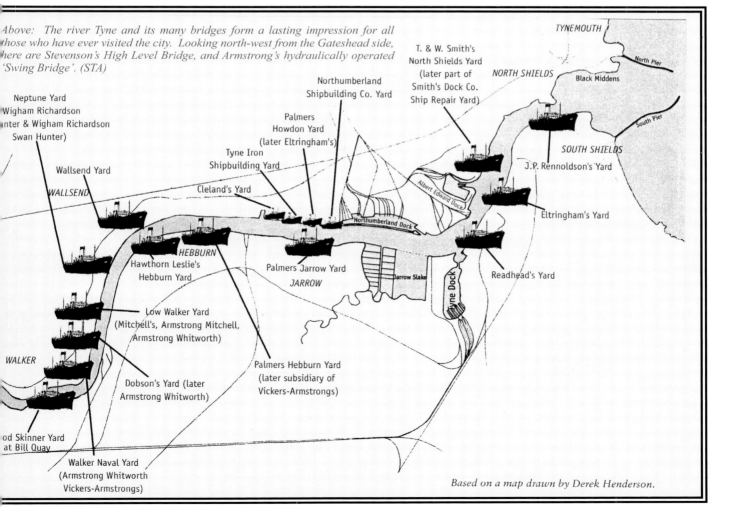

Above: The river Tyne and its many bridges form a lasting impression for all those who have ever visited the city. Looking north-west from the Gateshead side, here are Stevenson's High Level Bridge, and Armstrong's hydraulically operated 'Swing Bridge'. (STA)

Neptune Yard
Wigham Richardson
nter & Wigham Richardson
Swan Hunter)

Wallsend Yard

WALLSEND

Cleland's Yard

HEBBURN

Hawthorn Leslie's
Hebburn Yard

Low Walker Yard
(Mitchell's, Armstrong Mitchell,
Armstrong Whitworth)

WALKER

Dobson's Yard (later
Armstrong Whitworth)

od Skinner Yard
at Bill Quay

Walker Naval Yard
(Armstrong Whitworth
Vickers-Armstrongs)

Palmers Hebburn Yard
(later subsidiary of
Vickers-Armstrongs)

Palmers Jarrow Yard

JARROW

Tyne Iron
Shipbuilding Yard

Palmers
Howdon Yard
(later Eltringham's)

Northumberland
Shipbuilding Co. Yard

Jarrow Slake

Northumberland Dock

Albert Edward Dock

Tyne Dock

T. & W. Smith's
North Shields Yard
(later part of
Smith's Dock Co.
Ship Repair Yard)

NORTH SHIELDS

TYNEMOUTH

North Pier

Black Middens

South Pier

SOUTH SHIELDS

J.P. Rennoldson's Yard

Eltringham's Yard

Readhead's Yard

Based on a map drawn by Derek Henderson.

This Sunbeam/NCB trolleybus is kept in pristine condition in the later livery of Maidstone Corporation. It is shown here as seen in 2009 at the Sandtoft Trolleybus Museum. *(David Cole)*

1 – Creation

The Company Origins

Over the centuries the north east of England has been a major source of innovation and invention in many fields, in particular engineering and transport. The contribution to the development of ships and railways is well known as we have just read in pages 10/11, but developments in motor vehicles have been much more modest until the comparatively recent opening in the 1980s of the Nissan car plant at Washington, in Sunderland. The large-scale construction of commercial motor vehicle bodywork did not feature in the region, with one notable exception.

Northern Coachbuilders Ltd, of Newcastle upon Tyne, very soon after coming into existence had ambitions to become a national supplier of bodywork for commercial vehicles, buses and coaches. The origins of this company arose from an unlikely source, tea.

Samuel Smith, born in Leeds in 1872, was the epitome of the 'rags to riches' story. He began work as a butcher's errand boy when he was only nine years old. He then joined a Leeds tea firm, where sheer enthusiasm and hard work saw his position in the company rise rapidly, until he became one of their senior salesmen. His employers introduced the then novel idea of selling tea using a door-to-door delivery service in the 1890s. In 1907 at the age of 35 Smith decided to set up on his own behalf, but because of a working contract agreement he was obliged to leave the district. So, with his wife and six children all under nine years of age he 'upped sticks' and started his own business in Newcastle upon Tyne. Mr Watson and Mr Titterington joined him from his old firm. They acquired premises in Newcastle, where their carefully selected purchases of tea were blended and packed for sale. By abbreviating Titterington's name, they called the company 'Rington's Tea'. From the start, the business was based on the 'door-to-door' sales principle, which continues

How it all began. This beautifully detailed Rington's tea delivery van exhibited the skills available when Sam Smith established his fleet of delivery vans. The crafts of coachbuilders, blacksmiths, wheelwrights, glaziers, coach painters and signwriters are all demonstrated here. Just add a horse.
(Courtesy Ringtons)

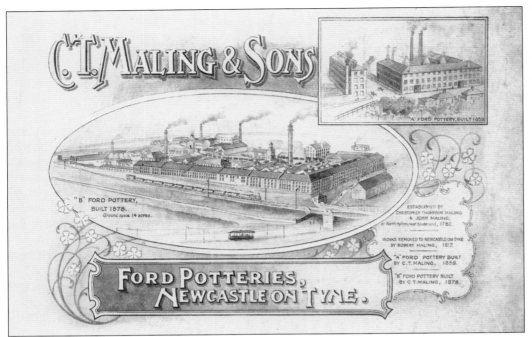

The manufacture of pottery in Tyneside has already been referred to on page 11, though most people would probably associate the other Newcastle with this type of production. One such company was CT Maling and Sons who, coincidentally, supplied teapots, cups and saucers to Ringtons for sale from their vans. Malings also produced special commemorative items. It was the loss of Ringtons' contract that was a contributory factor to Maling's closure in 1963. *(Courtesy Josie Hetherington)*

to this day, and before long it became a limited company, Ringtons Ltd. A fleet of horse drawn two-wheel vans was built up, and became a familiar sight around Tyneside. After the end of the 1914-18 war, sales improved rapidly, Ringtons quickly became a major supplier and blender of teas in the north of England and the Scottish borders. To cope with this the company began at first the repair, and then also the manufacture of the by now famous tea vans. At the Shields Road, Newcastle workshop, the striking black, green and gold vans were built, repaired and maintained in immaculate condition, creating a powerful sales symbol in addition to their task as delivery vehicles. The authors were quoted 1926 as the date when this activity began, but there is photographic evidence to indicate that this activity may have begun much

This Albion van of 1924 shows the established and distinctive Ringtons branding which was shared with the horse vans, motor vans and in this case, delivery of bulk supplies from Newcastle to the distribution depots. The livery was a basic black background with lime green relief and gold script. It is quite possible that Ringtons own coachbuilders produced the body as it features similar glazing around the top of the body to that of the horse vans. *(Courtesy Ringtons)*

earlier, from the time of the formation of the company. It is probable that their very first 'pony' vans were built and serviced at the Ringtons premises in Third Avenue, Heaton, Newcastle. A team of skilled coachbuilders and wheelwrights was created for this work, and from the 1920s the construction of motor vans was undertaken. These were clearly based on the same designs as those of the horse vans, and some may even have been conversions. The availability of cheap motor vans from the large motor manufacturers in the 1930s meant an end to such constructions, and Ringtons built up a fleet of quarter-ton Ford vans for use on the longer delivery rounds in country areas. They were painted in the now familiar Ringtons livery, though most urban areas continued to be served by the horse-drawn vans, such was their publicity value.

The economics of horse powered vehicles were very much in their favour for these duties. The advent of World War 2 severely affected Ringtons, however, due to the rationing of tea and government restrictions on its distribution. The company was forced to sell the horses, and the vans were placed in storage for the duration. After the war around half a dozen NCB battery-electric vans were adopted for some deliveries, but gradually most of the familiar horse vans were replaced by Ford motor vans. The last was retired in 1954, and may be seen on display at the North of England Open Air Museum at Beamish, in County Durham.

Sam Smith, never one to let the grass grow under his feet, noted the beginning of the decline of the horse van fleet in 1930, and looked for an opportunity to find suitable employment for his team of coachbuilders. The small vans for his own needs could be delivered from the motor manufacturers complete in primer paint for a fraction of the cost of building them in house. Contracts were found to build a few horse vans and small motor vans for outside customers. The problem was that there were plenty of small coachbuilding firms doing the same kind of work, but Smith spotted a gap in the market. Though there were exceptions, most of the large commercial vehicle, bus and coach bodies in the region were built elsewhere, in fact the nearest quantity and quality coachbuilders were in Yorkshire and Scotland. Smith had the premises, he had the skilled labour and he had the capital, and he decided to begin a new and separate enterprise.

The modern image, seen in 2013, as one of the Company's distinctively lettered vans stands outside the Publisher's Glossop Headquarters on a wet September day whilst making its regular bi-weekly deliveries of tea in the area. There are currently some 215 vans in the Ringtons fleet performing this service. (John A Senior)

2 – Inauguration

Beginning a New Venture

With a capital of £4,000, and Company Registration Number 261146, Northern Coachbuilders Ltd was incorporated on 16th December 1931. It was, according to the documents, 'to carry on the business of bus, lorry, tractor and motor garage proprietors and warehousemen etc.' The Directors were S Smith of The Grove, Gosforth, Northumberland, and S Smith (Jnr) of Jesmond Vale Terrace, Jesmond, Newcastle on Tyne. The company was a wholly owned subsidiary of Ringtons Ltd, who provided the funding. In 1933 the capital was increased to £6,700 and Samuel Smith (Junior) was confirmed as Managing Director, with a workforce of 30 employees based at premises in Shields Road. Another Ringtons company, Cut-Out (Cartons) Ltd, who made the cartons and packaging for Ringtons tea, shared the building. One of the first actions of the new company, quickly recognised as 'NCB', was to incorporate the existing business of GR Haugh, a local builder of heavy goods vehicle bodies. Haugh, whose repair shop in Fenkle Street also passed to NCB, had been established for some years in Newcastle with premises at St. Mary's Place, Northbold Road and Lovane Crescent at various times, and was also engaged in the haulage business. A large Haugh's van body on the first Halley 4½ton 'overtype' chassis was built in 1922 for Hunter's the bakers to make daily bulk deliveries of 2,412 loaves of bread on trays from the bakery in Gateshead to Stockton-on-Tees. Haugh joined

Just under half-sized reproduction of a tea carton produced by Cut-Out (Cartons) Ltd and showing the origins of the Company being used to good advantage. *(Geoff Burrows collection)*

NCB as a semi-independent coachbuilder and for some years concentrated on repair work and commercial vehicle bodies. For a number of years all NCB documents included the words 'Incorporating George R Haugh', while an area of the factory was set aside to build Haugh bodies. Haugh's had built horse-drawn carts and vans during the early part of the twentieth century, and was also engaged in the haulage business.

Northern Coachbuilders became sole agents in Northumberland and the northern part of Durham county for Reo vehicles, and this resulted in a number of orders for cabs and bodies for trucks, vans, buses and coaches. Many of these were mounted on the popular REO Speedwagon chassis, and were supplied to some familiar north east transport fleets such as Clarkson's and Smiles 'for Miles'. The output included a number of articulated and tipper lorries, some of these were used for coal delivery, understandably a major industry in the area. Minories Ltd, a Newcastle agent for the Rootes Group, established a relationship with NCB during this period, and as a result many Commer and Karrier chassis were given NCB bodies for local users. Travelling shops were a feature often seen in rural districts in the 1930s, and a fine specimen was built for Carrick's Cakes on a Commer chassis in 1934.

Work began in 1934 on a new airfield for Newcastle Corporation at Woolsington, about six miles north of the city. This is, of course, now known as Newcastle Airport, from where many internal and international commercial flights are made every day. In 1935 NCB supplied the first fire tender to the aerodrome; CBB 705 was based on a Reo chassis, built to the requirements of the Air Ministry, who dealt with such matters then.

At about this time Sam Smith took an interest in Domestos, a household bleach that had until then been sold in small quantities from a handcart in weekly markets around the north east. The originator was a man named Handley, and Sam Smith gave him business advice and financial assistance to set up the manufacturing plant. Under Smith's guidance, Domestos was soon nationally recognised, and NCB initially built many of the vans needed

17

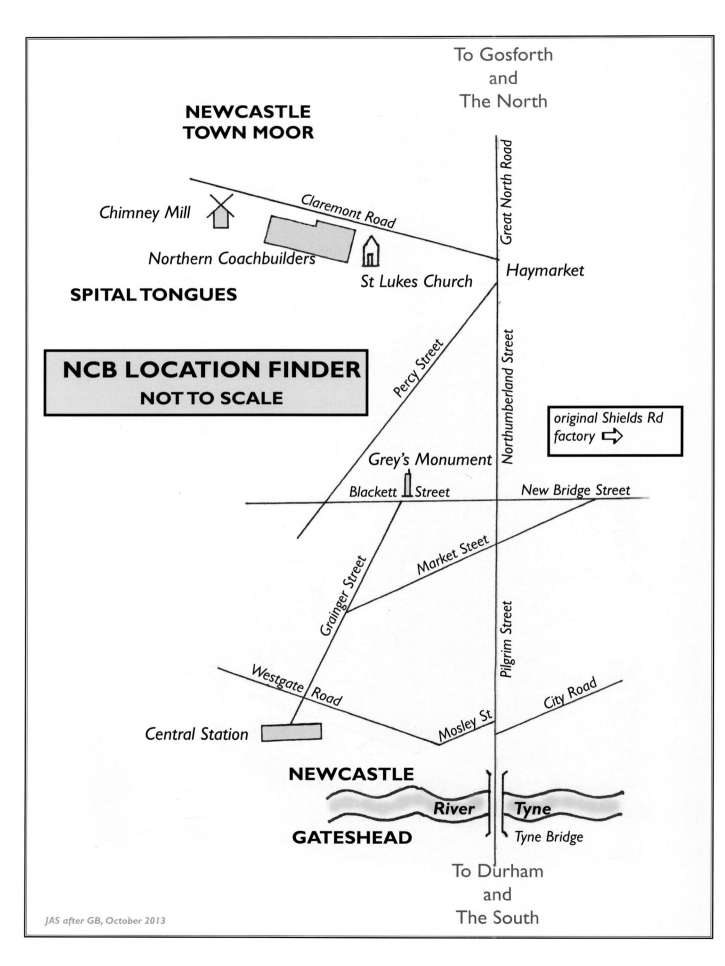

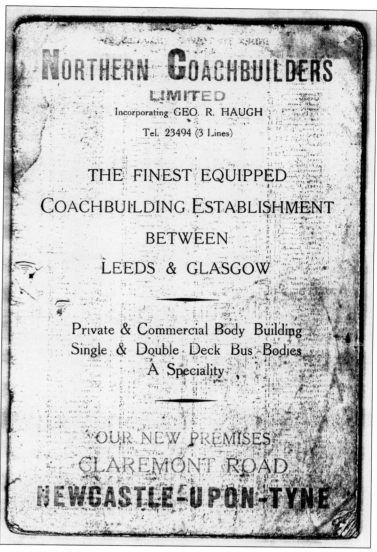

to distribute it around the country. Domestos went on to follow the example of Ringtons and began to build their own bodywork.

The first bus bodies known to have been built by NCB were for the Newcastle upon Tyne Education Committee. The initial vehicle, AVK 305, of conventional design with 20 wooden perimeter seats and the entrance alongside the driver on a normal-control Commer Centaur chassis, left the factory in March 1934. A second bus was then ordered to the same design, and BBB 310 was delivered in July. The same year saw the first NCB coach bodies, UP 8965/6 were constructed on Leyland Lion LT5A chassis for Wilkinson of Sedgefield. These two 32-seat forward-entrance coaches incorporated roof luggage compartments emblazoned with the legend 'Pullman Lounge'. Prominently displayed on the sides were boards lettered 'Radio Express'. Similar in style to a Burlingham-bodied coach supplied to the same fleet in 1933, they were regarded as the flagships of the Wilkinson fleet and employed on their West Hartlepool to Blackpool summer express service.

This photograph of the framework for the first NCB single-deck buses for Newcastle shows the initial one mounted on trestles before being lifted onto the Daimler COS4 chassis. Each component was carefully lettered and numbered for ease of assembly. Known as WAS patent construction, this all-steel design was made by Strachans (Successors) Ltd, of Acton, London. Recognising the burgeoning market for metal-framed body kits, Strachans attempted to 'get in on the act' with their own version, and in 1935 NCB bought five for the Newcastle contract. They became Nos. 169-173 (BTN 169-173), with rear-entrance 32-seat bodies, and survived in service (latterly with United) until 1950. Little else is known about the 'WAS' structures, and the venture appears to have been quietly abandoned by Strachans. *(JH Herdman collection)*

This official Metro-Cammell view of one of their single-deckers, 164, BTN 104, is included for comparison and shows that the positioning of the side indicator arrangement gave an immediate point of reference between the NCB bodies and those from the Birmingham manufacturer. Readers will see other differences, particularly in the positioning of items of the livery. *(D Slater collection)*

The first of many **NCB** orders for Newcastle Corporation was for five Daimler single-deckers with 34-seat rear-entrance bodies. The order for 10 Daimler chassis was shared with Metro-Cammell, who built the other five bodies using their patented steel framework. By positioning the side destination box further forward, it was easier and safer for the conductor to reach the winding handles. All 10 buses were sold to United Automobile Services in 1938 and had a long life, including re-engining with **AEC** petrol engines, and running on producer gas during part of World War 2. These photographs were taken at Newcastle Corporation's Byker works. (*James Riddell*)

The first **NCB** public service vehicles were a pair of 'radio coaches' built in 1934 for T Wilkinson of Sedgefield, Co Durham, one of which (UP 8965) is seen here. The body design was clearly based on that of a Burlingham-bodied Leyland Tiger TS6 (UP 7862) delivered to Wilkinson's the previous year. The chassis were the compact Leyland Lion LT5a model, and even though fitted with a four-cylinder petrol engine they must have coped well enough with the Pennine hills on their West Hartlepool to Blackpool service, for after some body attention the coaches remained in the fleet until the late 1940s.
(J Gibson collection)

NCB also became involved in the repair and rebuilding of buses and coaches, and numbers of commercial vehicles also began to arrive at NCB for renovation. NCB advertised that it was prepared to supply motor car bodies, but it is not clear how much of this work was done by the company. In 1934 a body was built on a 20/25hp Rolls-Royce chassis for managing director Sam Smith, who donated the car in 1939 to the Corbridge Home Ambulance Service, after it had been suitably converted.

Two more Commer buses (BVK 700, CTN 618) were built for the Newcastle Education Committee in 1935, but the big event of the year

This was Sam Smith's personal car, a 1934 Rolls Royce 20/25hp model. It carried the registration BBB 705. It has provincial rather than London coachwork and therefore Northern Coachbuilders may have built it. *(K Price collection)*

was the receipt of the first order from a municipal bus operator. Ten Daimler bus chassis were ordered by Newcastle upon Tyne Corporation Transport, and the contract for the all-metal bodywork was divided equally between the Metropolitan Carriage & Wagon Co Ltd (MCCW) of Birmingham, and Northern Coachbuilders. The NCB bodies each cost £558, a little less than the MCCW versions. The similarity between the products of the two bodybuilders can be judged from the views on pages 20 and 21. MCCW had designed and patented its own metal body framework, but Strachans of Acton supplied the steel framework kits for the NCB bodies, to their patented 'WAS' design. The finished 32-seat rear-entrance bodies were a credit to the fledgling coachbuilder, and survived in service until 1950.

The Daimler chassis for these buses were unique, in that they were the only ones of that marque to be fitted with Armstrong-Saurer four-cylinder diesel engines. Armstrong-Saurer Commercial Vehicles Ltd had been established in Scotswood, Newcastle as a subsidiary of the giant Armstrong-Whitworth company. The engines were made there under licence from the famous Saurer company of Switzerland, and the Daimler chassis were identified as type COS4.

The first mention of a Bedford receiving an NCB bus or coach body occurs in 1935. R Chisholm of Craghead in Co Durham, trading as 'The Diamond' in partnership with others, took a 26-seater bus body fitted to a Bedford WTL chassis. This was actually one of the range of Bedford lorry chassis, but the practise of using goods chassis for buses and coaches was by no means uncommon in the 1930s.

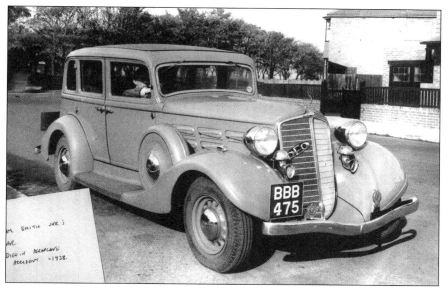

Northern Coachbuilders held a REO dealership for commercial vehicle chassis in the early 1930s and this magnificent 1934 model REO Flying Cloud limousine was run by the managing director, Sam Smith Jnr, who, as recorded later, was killed in 1938 in a flying accident. From this time onward his younger brother Malcolm would be managing the firm's business affairs.

The REO name arose from the initials of RE Olds who had set up the Oldsmobile motor company in the USA and after leaving it, set up REO to compete. Car production ceased in 1936 with the Airstream model but REO commercials continued for many years and the 1920s REO 'Speed Wagon' was a popular bus and lorry chassis in Britain. *(Bob Kell collection)*

Reo Motors (Britain) Ltd assembled US and Canadian chassis offering 6-cylinder engines, reliabliity and good performance. As British manufacturers caught up with Reo, NCB relinquished the tie. The Silkburn Coal Co BVK 705, carrying the NCB tradeplate 226 BB, below, was a 1935 REO 'Speed Wagon' articulated lorry, and the low height implies that it was used for distributing bagged coal. See also page 31. *(James Riddell)*

These five 1935 REO Speed Wagon 3ton tippers had 6-cylinder petrol engines and were built for *Smiles for Miles* of Blucher, Northumberland. They were photographed in Claremont Road with Newcastle Town Moor in the background, a location used for many official NCB photographs. *(James Riddell)*

3 – Expansion

The Move to Claremont Road

Space was now at a premium in the Shields Road factory, the large single-decker buses filled the workshop, leaving little room for other work, and there was insufficient height to consider the manufacture of double-deckers. The answer was found by acquiring a prime site in Claremont Road, at Spital Tongues on the western side of the famous Newcastle Town Moor, and it was here that a completely new factory was built in 1936. Initially 10,000 sq ft in size, the site was developed at a capital outlay of £250,000. A fuel filling station was situated at the front of the new plant adjacent to the road, and a large concrete canopy bearing the name of the company surmounted this. The name was repeated on the wall underneath the canopy, and interestingly the clause 'Incorporating George R Haugh' was placed underneath. Adjacent to the factory stood Chimney Mill built in 1782, but the opportunity to use this in the company publicity was never taken. Instead, the term 'Claremont Coachwork' was used.

The original factory in Shields Road was retained and continued to be used by Cut-Outs Ltd, whose business also expanded to include the supply of packaging to other businesses. One of the biggest customers was Thomas Hedley Ltd, Newcastle soap manufacturers and suppliers, later to become part of the Proctor & Gamble group. From this time Cut-Outs was less dependent on the tea packaging, which became one of the smaller requirements.

Once established in the new Claremont Road factory, NCB production expanded quickly, though unfortunately the records have not survived. Of the commercial vehicles, output ranged from small Ford and Morris vans right through the ranges up to three and four-axle heavy lorries on chassis such as the AEC Mammoth Major. The Gateshead baker Hunter's took some vans including the popular half-ton Morris C30/F, a semi-forward control model with the engine offset to the nearside, in the manner of bus chassis. Bainbridge's,

This is the impressive façade and canopy of the new NCB Claremont Road factory in 1938, seen with the ancient windmill behind. This structure had been designed by John Smeaton who is perhaps more famous for having also designed the Eddystone Lighthouse. Vehicles drawn up include, from the left, a Riley and an MG saloon car. Under the canopy are FVK 19, a Bedford van for Domestos; JR 7907, a Commer van for Truetime Deliveries; and a Ringtons tea van. Outside are a Leyland Lynx 4/5 ton lorry (GR 5400) for Hepplewhite & Shaw of Sunderland; and two Bedford 'Parcels Express' vans for United Automobile Services together with further unidentified lorries. *(James Riddell)*

a large Newcastle department store, became a regular customer for three-quarter ton Ford and Commer vans. The repair and replacement of lorry bodies continued, as did the work required to maintain the Ringtons tea vans in pristine condition. It is difficult to determine the extent of the work carried out because NCB had earned an enviable reputation for fine coachpainting, and it is believed that many of the vehicles that passed through the Claremont Road works were only there for that purpose.

An interesting vehicle was built in 1936, in that it was battery-electric powered. The little half-ton van, DTN 816, was mounted on a chassis built by Midland Electric Vehicles Ltd for NESCo, the local electricity company in the north east. It could not have been foreseen at the time that eventually the manufacture of complete battery-electric vehicles would become one of the principal NCB products.

Now that the company had the available space, quite a number of furniture vans were built, large and handsome vehicles on all manner of chassis including Leyland Lions. Hoults of Newcastle realised the practicality of these low framed bus chassis, and took two, in 1936 and 1937. One of these (DTN 240) found itself in a clandestine operation at the beginning of the war in 1939, when it was requisitioned by the government and used to transport valuable artefacts and important documents to secret places of storage for the duration of the conflict. Hoults also bought some similar bodies mounted on the smaller companion chassis, the Leyland Cub.

Although the company could still be called a 'jobbing' coachbuilder at this stage, in other words willing and able to accept work for almost anything on wheels, it was gradually moving towards a more stable existence. This was realised by the number of contracts for fleets of vehicle bodywork now being received. One such customer was the London & North Eastern Railway Company (LNER), which returned to NCB several times for batches of dropside lorries on Fordson 'Sussex' three-axle chassis. The largest of these LNER

The significance of this vehicle could not have been guessed when it was built in 1936 for the North Eastern Electricity Supply Company. The battery-electric chassis was built by the Midland Electric Vehicle Co Ltd, and the NCB van body was used for a variety of purposes. No doubt much publicity was gained from the link between the battery power and the electricity company. Notice that the new style maker's board now incorporates the wording *Claremont Coachwork* above the company name and address. *(James Riddell)*

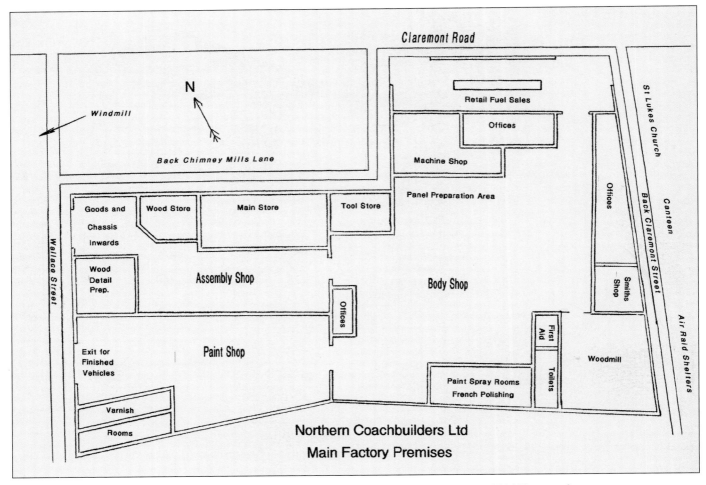

The **Northern Coachbuilders** factory in Claremont Road was established in 1936 with a floor space of 10,000 square feet. This drawing shows the works in 1945 at its maximum of 73,200 square feet after several extensions, Not shown is the mezzanine floor above the wood detailing area and goods inwards. This contained the office of the **Chief Engineer** and the design and drawing offices. Another mezzanine floor extended above the three stores, where the trim shop (upholstery), drawing store and print room were located. *(Geoff Burrows)*

Pre-war **NCB** advertisements seem thin on the ground but these two appeared around 1938/9. The original view of the Thornycroft lorry appears on page 30. *(Geoff Burrows collection)*

This view of the interior of the Claremont Road factory was taken in the spring of either 1936 or 1937, and is full of interesting vehicles. From the left foreground can be seen the Morris-Commercial company lorry; two Ringtons tea vans (Nos. 5 & 97); a small Triumph car and Sam Smith senior's car, believed to have been bodied by NCB themselves. Specifically moved in on the left for the photograph are a small Bedford or Commer bus; two 'Triumph' type bodies, probably on TSM chassis; then three Leyland Tiger coaches for refurbishment for the Young's of South Shields 'Always Ready' fleet; of which the nearest UW 7690, is a TS1 model; and also CU 2603/4, which had been re-registered from DH 6615/6 after purchase from the Bloxwich Transport Co in 1930. On trestles beyond the large unidentified van is a bus body of which nothing is known other than it appears to have originated on an AEC Regal chassis, by the evidence of the visible autovac tank. NCB coachbuilders were versatile! (*James Riddell*)

A second municipal operator became an NCB customer in 1936. South Shields Corporation bought two Daimler COG5s with 32-seat forward-entrance bus bodies. They were similar to Weymann-bodied Daimlers already in the South Shields fleet. *(James Riddell)*

Left: A third, identical bus, CU 3793, was built in 1937. This 1953 view shows it following a rebuild in the Corporation workshops in 1951. The lower edge of the indicator box has been modified, presumably to aid the driver's vision. The waistrail mouldings have also been removed. *(Geoff Burrows)*

orders was for no less than 50 bodies. The Durham and north eastern area collieries continued to request numbers of tipper lorries for local domestic coal delivery. Amongst the customers to be served with bodywork built in the new facilities was United Automobile Services Ltd, which stripped the fire-damaged Vickers 32-seat bus body from a 1929 Thornycroft BC chassis (EF 4232), then sent it to NCB to be fitted with a parcel van body.

A final Commer bus was built for the Newcastle Education Authority in 1936 (DTN 596), but a new customer for buses appeared on the scene in that year. Darlington Triumph Services had previously designed and built most of their own bodies in their Darlington coach works. Their services were expanding rapidly, and they were unable to build new bodies quickly enough to meet the increased demand, and sent their 1929 Leyland Tiger (HN 6676) for a replacement 34-seat rear-entrance bus body. Evidently pleased, NCB became their preferred supplier for the bodies that they were unable to build themselves. Triumph ordered a batch of seven TSM HA39A7 chassis in 1936/7. NCB built the bodies for two of the three 1936 models (BHN 903/9), and the third (BHN 948) had a Triumph body. All four of the 1937 coaches were built by NCB (CHN 887/932/995, DHN 102), and a similar coach for JJ Baker of Quarrington Hill, Co Durham (BUP 805). TSM was the manufacturer formerly known as

This picture is believed to be the first **NCB** bus built for Darlington Triumph. The clue is given by the oval nameplate on the ground, used before production moved to Spital Tongues, where a rectangular plate bearing the words 'Claremont Coachwork' was used, as mentioned previously. The distinctive **TSM** radiator projects forward, just like the later Guy Arabs. *(James Riddell)*

Centre: Furniture vans became an **NCB** speciality, and DTN 240 was one of two for the Newcastle removal firm Hoults, mounted on a Leyland Lion **LT7** passenger chassis to give a low loading base. This vehicle was seconded to the government during World War 2 as mentioned in the text. *(James Riddell)*

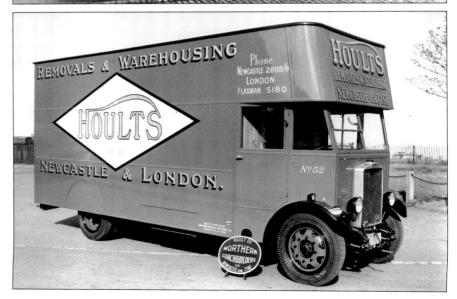

Lower: A smaller Hoult furniture van is shown on a forward-control Leyland Cub 3ton chassis. Again, to achieve a low-loading line this is probably an **SKP** chassis of 1933/4. The registration identity of the van is not known. *(James Riddell)*

Tilling Stevens Motors, but its association with the Tilling organisation ended in 1930, causing the need for a change of name.

The NCB bodies were closely based on the Triumph designs, though there were detail differences. Confusion has arisen over the identity of the manufacturers of these bodies among observers in the past, particularly in view of the fact that there are no remaining official NCB records. The authors believe that the details shown in this book reflect the true situation.

As well as constructing new bodies for buses and coaches, NCB carried out repairs and rebuilding of older vehicles. Three known examples were early Leyland Tiger coaches for Young's of South Shields. All were second hand to the Young's fleet, and the work was considerable, indeed one of them was given a normal rigid roof in place of a soft canvas topped roof, and all three were given sliding heads, known in those days as 'sunshine roofs'.

A second municipal operator became an NCB customer in 1936. South Shields Corporation bought two Daimler COG5s (CU 3569/70), with 32-seat forward-entrance bus bodies. The appearance was similar to that of four Weymann-bodied Daimlers already in the South Shields fleet, though with more rake to the front and more curvature at the rear end. A third identical bus (CU 3793) was built by NCB for South Shields in 1937.

Bell's Services Ltd of Westerhope, near Newcastle, bought an NCB 32-seat rear-entrance coach body, mounted on an AEC Regal II, model 0862 chassis (JR 5091) in 1936. Well balanced and restrained in style, one of its features was a nicely shaped roof mounted luggage rack. The design was clearly related to

Claremont Coachwork lettering as displayed on the window of a finished vehicle.

NCB gained a number of contracts from the LNER for goods vehicle bodies, and FS 6317 is from a 1938 batch. The chassis has been lengthened with twin axles to allow the carriage of bulkier loads. As modified, the vehicle was designated a Fordson Sussex, and the LNER livery was a deep purple-blue that was remarkably resistant to dirt and inattention. *(James Riddell)*

This Thornycroft short wheelbase Sturdy model has been built up as a 5ton tipper, probably for demonstration purposes. Used for publicity, this photograph shows a vehicle believed to have been sold to Hewitt's of Morpeth, Northumberland. *(James Riddell)*

Some of Newcastle Corporation's large batch of AEC model 411 buses of 1925 had long lives. One such was TN 1047, which was withdrawn from passenger service in 1938 and sent to NCB for conversion into a tower wagon for the Newcastle & Gateshead Gas Co Ltd, and then saw nearly ten further years of use. The chassis was shortened, and the front half of the Strachan & Brown body was retained for use as a crew cab and tool store. At some time, probably during the early 1930s, the driver's cab had been modernised with the replacement of the original AEC dash panel. *(James Riddell)*

This REO Speed Wagon was one of the first commercial vehicles built by NCB on the US 6-cylinder chassis. ATN 88 would be a 3ton tipper and was new in December 1933/January 1934. William Leech went on to become a major north-east housebuilder until the early 1990s. *(James Riddell)*

The streamlined cab of this late 1930s Foden DG was a product of the chassis builder, making these most identifiable and memorable lorries. The sturdy flatbed body was built by NCB for Mutter Howey, a Scottish haulier, who maintained a Newcastle depot. As an 8-wheeler with double drive it would almost certainly have a Gardner 6LW engine. NCB was also noted for its coachpainting, typified here by the smart blue livery with gilded signwriting and red chassis. *(James Riddell)*

31

the bodies built for Triumph. Bell's Services sold out to United in 1937, and JR 5091 became ARO35 in that fleet. United then re-modelled the side panels and mouldings, to give the coach the 'United' appearance of its fleet of front line coaches. It was also given an enlarged destination indicator.

The first order for double-deckers came in 1937 when Newcastle Corporation sent five Daimler COG5 chassis to Claremont Road. It is believed that metal framework supplied by Accles & Pollock may have been used, though the authors have been unable to confirm this. These somewhat angular buses were built to the exacting specification of TP Easton, the Newcastle General Manager. A ventilation system patented by him was included, in an attempt to clear the tobacco-laden atmosphere caused by the Geordie desire to travel with all the windows closed. The method consisted of wire mesh-covered apertures at the front of both decks, connected to horizontal tubular handrails running the length of the decks at ceiling level. These had small holes drilled at intervals along their length through which fresh air emerged. The rear end of the tubes was closed off, and the system was quite effective. Smartly finished in the very dark navy blue Newcastle livery, 187-191 (EBB 187-191) had contrasting cream bands and gold lining.

Somewhat disappointingly, Newcastle did not immediately award a repeat order, but returned to its favourite supplier, MCCW. NCB was not short of work however, and by 1938 the new factory had grown in size from 10,000 square feet to 73,200. This included the addition of new areas for finishing work and a purpose designed paint shop and varnish room.

Fred Robinson of Stockton-on-Tees, a long-time haulier and operator of AEC charabancs, built up a sizeable fleet of Albion lorries in the mid-1930s. UP 8567 was one of the first, in December 1933 with an NCB flat bed. It was a 6ton M550 model and petrol engined. *(James Riddell)*

Facing page: The first NCB order for double-deckers came in 1937 when Newcastle Corporation sent five Daimler COG5 chassis to Claremont Road. The painted registration number on the glass, illuminated at night by the saloon lighting, was a common characteristic at the time, though it was unusual to find more than one rear lamp. *(James Riddell)*

This splendid broadside view shows the elegant lines of the coach on an AEC Regal II for Bell's Services Ltd   *(James Riddell)*

The enlarged factory required an increase in the workforce, which now numbered about 150. Skilled coachbuilders and associated tradesmen came from a number of sources, possibly the furthest were from Alexander's of Stirling, and Cowieson of Glasgow. There were sufficient people from 'north of the border' to provide a team for NCB 'Geordies v. Scots' football matches at weekends. Other staff came from the luxury coachbuilder FW Plaxton of Scarborough, where the work tended to be seasonal in demand.

Apparently satisfied with the parcel van body supplied in 1936, United followed this up in 1938 with an order for four new NCB parcel delivery vans on Bedford WTL bus chassis. These smart streamlined vans (DHN 870-3) were built to a United design, and became a familiar sight in the north east, making daily domestic and commercial deliveries throughout the region. United was one of several bus companies which capitalised on the fact that small to medium sized parcels could be carried quickly from town to town by bus, then taken directly to the recipient's door by parcel van. In doing this, they were many years ahead of today's 'Interlink' vans.

Amongst the special vehicles built in 1938 was a demonstration van body on a Commer chassis for British Ropes Ltd, and a Bedford horsebox for the famous Topham family to transport their racehorses. The Tophams were based in Masham in the North Riding of Yorkshire, so it can be seen that the reputation of NCB bodywork was beginning to spread further from the immediate area of Tyneside.

Another market explored by the company was one receiving growing interest from the public, trailer caravans, and one was built in 1938, but this activity was not actively pursued. The name 'Wakefield's Caravans' has been quoted to the authors as either a manufacturer taken over by NCB or a name under which they would have been sold. The outline was similar to most other caravans being built at that time. Design work was resumed in 1945, but abandoned in 1948. It would seem that there was little enthusiasm in the company for attempting the production of such a specialised product.

Commercial vehicle work continued to run at a satisfactory level. The Newcastle store and removals firm Currie's bought three furniture van bodies on Foden chassis, and a Thornycroft chassis was chosen by Cameron of West Hartlepool for the carriage of their world famous (in the north east!) ales.

Though the authors know that caravan drawings were being prepared at NCB following World War II, this pre-war photograph is the only evidence that a caravan was ever completed by NCB. As more motor cars capable of the task of towing heavy caravans became available, the popularity of 'caravanning' during the 1930s grew quickly. Apparently NCB was interested in becoming a caravan manufacturer, to add to its other coachbuilding skills. The design was completely conventional, and appears to have no features that could not be found in other contemporary caravans. Note the spindly car jacks supporting the van for the photographer.
(Geoff Burrows collection)

Cameron's Lion Brewery in Hartlepool is still a going concern. Thornycroft GBB 832 was a 5 ton Sturdy model on 1938 and probably had a Gardner 4LK engine. GR Haugh built brewery wagons for Newcastle Breweries on Albion and Thornycroft chassis.
(James Riddell)

Most bus, and some tramway (including Gateshead), operators developed a parcel-carrying business well before today's 'white vans'. United Auto, based at Darlington, covered large areas of north Yorkshire, Durham and Northumberland and supplemented pick-up by scheduled buses with dedicated vans. NCB built four 'Goods Express' Bedford vans on WTL chassis registered DHN 570-3 in 1938 and numbered PB (Parcel Bedford) 59-62. PB61 is carrying NCB tradeplate 102 BB in the photograph. In 1948, with the nationalisation of road haulage, they were sold to British Road Services. *(Bob Kell collection)*

Northern Coachbuilders turned out this attractive van with coach styling mounted on a Commer N2 30cwt chassis for British Ropes Ltd in 1938. The clerestory roof, wheel trims and high quality of finish indicate that this was probably a sales or demonstration vehicle. *(James Riddell)*

NCB developed a strong link with Newcastle motor agents Minories Ltd, who sold Rootes Group products Humber, Hillman and Sunbeam-Talbot cars, and Commer and Karrier commercial vehicles. This is a 1938 furniture van for the Newcastle department store Bainbridge's, on a Commer LN4 4-ton chassis.
(James Riddell)

In addition to constructing new bodies for buses and coaches, NCB carried out repairs and rebuilding to older vehicles. Coaches had evolved slowly from the open charabanc of the mid-1920s to the 'open road' coach of 1930. Fresh air, and plenty of it, was still highly regarded and most coaches had a 'sliding head' of canvas which could be rolled back so that sun and wind could caress the happy traveller (at times!).

This Leyland Tiger with, originally it is believed, a dual-entrance London Lorries body, rapidly became unfashionable in the mid-1930s when more comfort was demanded. The Tiger chassis was reliable and fast so NCB updated the body with full roof (and sliding section only), luggage provision and single door entry, for Young of South Shields (trading as Ever Ready), who also commissioned NCB to modernise two more 1928 Leyland Tigers. Their previous identity was DH 6615/6 from the fleet of the Bloxwich Motor Transport Co. Unusually the 'new' coaches were re-registered in South Shields as CU 2603/4. The CU mark for South Shields vehicles had local support as (by chance or design) it recognised the Roman name attributed to the port, *Caer Urfa*, which was a major staging post to supply the garrisons on the Roman Wall.
(James Riddell)

Working and retired coal miners were eligible for free 'concessionary' coal, and this was delivered regularly in special narrow lorries to negotiate the 'back lanes' in the older mining villages. Removable dividers were fitted into these lorries to enable a three-quarter load to be tipped ('teemed' in the local vernacular) outside the miner's homes. The miners and their families were given until darkness fell to shovel the coal through a small hatch in the wall into their coal stores, or a charge was made for the next delivery. Karrier Motors built the chassis and cab of this **CK3** model, and **NCB** built the tipper body for Lambton, Hetton, Joicey Collieries Ltd in 1938. (*James Riddell*)

Sparks was a well respected baker and caterer on Tees-side and surrounding areas, and this pair of 1939 Commer delivery vans sparkle even on the rainy day of the photograph. NCB indicated its pride in them by fitting two makers' transfers, one on each side of the front dash panel. (*James Riddell*)

An almost forgotten manufacturer of lorry chassis in the 1930s was Arran Motors Ltd of Welwyn Garden City. In 1934 their 3ton oil-engined forward-control chassis cost £565. BPT 841 must have been one of the last chassis built and it was registered in March 1936, oddly, as a 'Gardner chassis' which implies that this Arran Diesel was Gardner (4LK?) engined. The reason for the anonymous livery was that the original owner was Northern Explosives of Haswell, Co Durham and the van would be used to deliver explosives to mines and quarries. No doubt an oil-engined chassis was specifically chosen for this work. (James Riddell)

The cab and dropside body on this AEC Mammoth Major, one of the largest lorries in production at the time, was built by NCB in 1939. The famous Newcastle United footballer, Stan Seymour, came from the same family as the customer, Seymour Bros of East Stanley, Co Durham. (James Riddell)

The Yorkshire (North Riding) County Council bought some Albion lorries with NCB bodywork. A Rootes Group motor distributor The Minories Ltd supplied a number of their customers with Commers and Karriers fitted with NCB bodywork of different types. Amongst the lorry chassis passing through the works during this period were Scammells, AECs and a rare Arran diesel. In January 1936 the latter received a van body designed for the carriage of explosives. Arran went out of business in 1935, so this chassis was amongst the last. The LNER provided another large order, on this occasion for demountable containers for use on both road and rail. This concept was popular at that time, being used in particular for the removal of household furniture from door to door over long distances.

In 1937/8 four of the Basingstoke-built Thornycroft Dainty, a passenger version of the Dandy lorry chassis with a high radiator and engine, were provided with full-fronted bodywork by NCB. Local stage operators took several; one (CPT 507) went to E Wheatley of Coundon, Co Durham. In rural Northumberland, Raisbeck of Bedlington bought a 26-seat bus, (JR 6165), Fish & Appleby of Choppington took similar JR 6166 and Foster of Otterburn a 24-seat coach registered JR 6319.

Below: In 1937/8 four of the prettily named but ruggedly constructed Thornycroft Dainty, a passenger version of the Dandy lorry chassis with a high radiator and engine, were provided with full-fronted bodywork by NCB. They all went to local bus and coach operators, and this is believed to be JR 6319 of Foster of Otterburn, Northumberland. *(James Riddell)*

39

4 – Consolidation

The Growth of the Business

Coach operators required vehicles that kept up with the fashions of the day. NCB began to compete in this market in about 1937, when the trend was towards streamlining, with curvaceous waistlines and polished mouldings to emphasise the effect. The Bedford chassis was already established as the market leader for coaches of 20-26 seat capacity. Standard body styles were shown in the chassis maker's publicity, built by Duple Motor Bodies of Hendon, London. Naturally, while many took advantage of the 'Bedford-Duple' sales package, some took a more individualistic approach on that and other makes of chassis.

FW Plaxton, situated some 80 miles away from NCB at Scarborough on the north Yorkshire coast, was becoming an important north regional coach body specialist. Plaxton designs incorporated shaped pillars with individually curved louvres over the side windows. During the years up to 1939, the coach designs of NCB and Plaxton on Bedford chassis were remarkably similar, suggesting possible migration of staff and ideas between the two builders. To the authors' knowledge, NCB built a total of eleven 26-seat coach bodies on the Bedford WTB semi-forward control chassis between 1937 and 1939. The first (EBB 349) went to The Eden of West Auckland in 1937, but no photographs have been found, and the body style is unknown. In 1938 two bodies with a steeply sloping front and windscreen were built. Only a small part of the bonnet was visible, and removable panels gave access to the bonnet. One, JR 8080, went to Tait of Morpeth and the other was GVK 414 for Frazer of Prudhoe. This

Below and Facing: The construction of the largest vehicle to date in 1938 was partly a trial. One of a batch of Guy BTX three-axle trolleybus chassis for Newcastle was shown at the 1937 Commercial Motor Show, and NCB was asked to build the 60-seat body for it. Metro-Cammell provided the steel framework, and NCB completed the vehicle with several distinguishing features including a Roe patent safety staircase and shaped convex waistrails. Finished in sparkling yellow, maroon and cream, Newcastle trolleybus 109 (FVK 109) entered service in 1938, but it was to remain unique.
(James Riddell both)

style closely resembled one of the current FW Plaxton coach designs from that company's Yorkshire factory.

Later that year the Bedford WTB was improved with a new engine, and the radiator was enclosed by a rounded grille that became very familiar on the subsequent Bedford OB and even the wartime OWB version. A coach body was built by NCB for display at the 1938 Scottish Motor Show; this was eventually registered HTN 133 and sold to Harris of Leven. Three further bodies of this type were built, JR 9689 for Moffitt of Acomb, and JR 9953/4 for Appleby & Jordan of Bedlington. Following the opening of Associated Coachbuilders (ACB) at Sunderland in 1946, several NCB employees went to work there. This may have had some bearing on the fact that ACB built at least 12 bodies for Bedford OB chassis that bore a close resemblance to this 1938 NCB version.

The final four NCB bodies on Bedford WTB chassis were supplied to Galley's Tours, of Newcastle, and the intermediate pillars, capped with polished aluminium, were very narrow. While this was an industry trend, the similarity with the contemporary Plaxton body is remarkable. With the absence of the production records of both firms, enthusiasts have had difficulty in ascribing the provenance of a number of late 1930s coach bodies. However, it is certain that no pre-war Bedford OB chassis received NCB bodies.

Returning to 1937, the stage was now set for a change of emphasis in the output of the company, one which was to lead to it becoming one of the well-known, if short-lived, names in the passenger transport industry. This was heralded by an order from Newcastle upon Tyne Corporation.

One of the exhibits at the 1937 Commercial Motor Show was one of a batch Guy BTX three-axle trolleybus chassis on order for Newcastle. After the close of the show, the chassis was sent to NCB, and MCCW supplied the structure for the 60-seat body. Constructed to the Newcastle standard trolleybus layout by Northern Coachbuilders, it had a normal open rear platform for the entrance, and a forward exit. Newcastle had on order a batch of Roe bodied buses, and

clearly approved of their patented double landing 'safety' staircase, because the new trolleybus was fitted with one of the same type at the rear, built under licence. The forward exit was equipped with a staircase of the pattern that was normal for Newcastle trolleybuses, and power operated folding doors under the control of the driver. The appearance of the exterior was similar in many respects to the trolleybuses already in service with Newcastle, though the shallow 'droop' of the front dome and the convex waistrails were identification features. The exterior was painted in Newcastle's trolleybus livery.

Northern Coachbuilders engineer Donald MacArthur and his Newcastle Corporation counterpart worked closely together on the design and production of the trolleybus. As could be expected there were a number of discussions over details, including some problems that had been found in Newcastle's earlier trolleybuses, (not, of course, NCB-bodied). Amicable agreement was reached on all points, and No. 109 (FVK109) was delivered in November 1938, entering service in the following month. In January 1939 council authorisation was given for £1,106 to be spent on the purchase of the body.

The biggest pre-war order received by NCB for bus bodies came from Newcastle Corporation in 1939 for 18 double-deck bodies on Daimler COG5 chassis. In contrast to their yellow trolleybus livery, Newcastle motor buses were painted in a very stately 'midnight' blue and cream, and their services were marketed as 'the blue buses'. A light adjacent to the destination box gave a blue illumination at night. These buses also subscribed to the north east practice of using headlamps in the position normally associated with foglamps. Frequent thick, choking fog arising from factory chimneys and domestic coal fires in virtually every house made this arrangement necessary. Three of these buses are seen posed in front of the imposing Claremont Road factory. *(James Riddell)*

Darlington Triumph Services changed its allegiance from TSM chassis to the Leyland Tiger in 1938, but stayed with NCB for the bodies. Three new Leyland Tiger TS8s (EHN 351/2, 653) received NCB bodies to a new design, and without the roof-mounted luggage rack. Coach seating for 35 passengers was featured, with overhead parcel racks. The straight waistrail was stepped up slightly after the five forward bays, with a gentle slope downward towards the back. Tapered pillars and curved louvres also featured.

A sad event in the history of the company took place in May 1938. The Managing Director Sam Smith junior was a flying enthusiast, and while flying his Percival Gull monoplane he crashed on Skiddaw in the Lake District. His brother Malcolm took his place at the company.

A significant order for Newcastle for 18 double-deck bodies was then received on Daimler COG5 chassis as with the 1937 contract. This time a very pleasing exterior shape was achieved with smoothly contoured front and rear profiles. The Newcastle specification again included the Roe patent staircase, and Easton's ventilation system. The authors believe that these NCB Daimlers

The splendid publicity photograph, taken on a carefully selected day to illustrate three of the 1939 Newcastle Daimlers, also clearly shows the distinctive canopy at the front of the factory topped with the enormous neon **NCB** sign, visible at night from a considerable distance, and the windmill in the background. Below, number 222 successfully passes its tilt test in an earlier view before the distinctive indicator blinds had been fitted to the vehicle. The table has been tilted to 28° but the Daimler is stable and the securing ropes in case of failure are not needed. More than half the weight of the vehicle is in the Gardner-engined chassis and double-deckers were not as unstable as they may appear.
(James Riddell)

Streamlined coachwork was in vogue during the later 1930s, and **NCB** produced several versions. This Bedford **WTB** carries a body illustrating the similarity between the **NCB** and Plaxton designs of 1938, suggesting possible movement of staff between the two firms. Access to the engine appears to have been severely compromised. Although the identity of the vehicle has not been established, it was very similar to JR 8080, an NCB-bodied Bedford **WTB** coach supplied to Tait's of Knowsgate, Northumberland. *(James Riddell)*

A new louvred radiator cowling was introduced in 1938 that was to become synonymous with Bedford chassis. It was fitted to the later **WTB** chassis, and was almost universal on **OB** and **OWB** buses and coaches. **NCB** displayed this attractive coach body at the 1938 Scottish Motor Show; in 1939 it was registered HTN 133 and sold to Harris of Leven, Fife. After appearing briefly in the Alexander fleet it later migrated back to English operators in the midlands and south-west. *(James Riddell)*

In 1939 Geo Galley of Newcastle ordered four Bedford **WTB** chassis with Plaxton bodies. They were of the 'pillarless' design with narrow pillars in the glazed area introduced for the 1939 season. This body is shown on a Dodge **SBF** chassis with Crowe Bros of Osmotherly in the North Riding. The Galley batch were HTN 662-5 delivered in May 1939 but they were requisitioned after a year or so and did not come back to Newcastle. HTN 662 is seen as a travelling shop in Great Houghton, Yorks in April 1956. The similarity to BAJ 943 is obvious and clearly HTN 662-5 had Plaxton bodies in design and specification but were they built in Scarborough? A lingering doubt remains as they were recorded by the late Bob Davis as NCB bodies. Bob lived in Newcastle, knew the NCB factory, visited Galleys (and knew they had other Bedford/Plaxton coaches) and recorded BAJ 943 as Plaxton. If Plaxton sub-contracted the Galley order to NCB, they must have provided the body drawings. No evidence of any formal link between Plaxton and NCB is known. Nearly all of NCB's coach bodies on Bedford chassis, however, went to operators north of Tyne. *(Bob Kell; Senior Transport Archive)*

were of two batches, one using composite construction and the other all-metal. At the time Accles & Pollock, a Tube Investments company, were actively promoting their tailor-made frameworks, supplied in kit form. Several major coachbuilders were supplied, each to their own recognisable designs. There is unconfirmed evidence that NCB may have received some of these kits for the Newcastle contract. What is certain is that the front corner pillars on some of the bodies were wider, and there were detail differences in the interiors of the two batches, suggesting that different methods of construction may have been used.

The completed buses were delivered between June 1939 and January 1940. They all received attention in the Byker Road works of Newcastle Corporation between 1946 and 1950. Some were given 'D' shaped windows at both ends of the lower deck at this time, probably to enclose strengthening body members. However, most retained their distinctive pointed end convex waistrails.

It is a matter of conjecture what the future would have held for the business relationship between NCB and Newcastle at that time, because it was not until 1942 that Newcastle made any further orders, when deciding post-war requirements. There were to be bus and trolleybus bodies from both MCCW and Roe, but the NCB name was absent. However, by the time that the war had ended their order book had been completely re-written, with several previously unused coachbuilders being added to the list of suppliers, and some additional chassis builders.

Darlington Triumph made a repeat order in 1939 for another three bodies on Leyland Tiger TS8 chassis (EHN 654-6), similar to their 1938 requirements. The coach seats in the Triumph vehicles were made in Claremont Road, and Triumph bought batches of similar seats from NCB for other buses in their fleet from time to time.

Wilkinson's of Sedgefield bought a Leyland Tiger TS8 (DUP 692) in 1939, this has been recorded by some as carrying an NCB coach body, but after careful deliberation the authors consider this to be Plaxton. Drawings were also made at NCB for new bodies to be fitted to the 1934 Wilkinson Leyland Lions, but there is no evidence to believe that this was carried through.

The country was now preparing for the possibility of war, and building contractors George Wimpey had won a large government contract for the construction of air raid shelters and reinforced concrete buildings to serve as control posts manned by air raid wardens. Indeed, it is now believed that the much-maligned 'Peace in our time' speech by Prime Minister Chamberlain in 1938 was crucial in gaining a year during which the country was able to begin preparations for the conflict to come. Wimpey's bought a number of NCB tippers mounted on Commer chassis.

E&N Ritchie of Hetton-le-Hole in Co Durham took a Thornycroft Sturdy equipped for general haulage in 1939. A new livestock transport body was fitted in 1953, this was altered in 1963 to become a coal delivery lorry. After retiring it in 1967 the family at first retained and then restored the vehicle to rally condition. There cannot be many 75 year old vehicles to have had only one owner from new.

The next large bus order to be received came from much further afield than any previous work for NCB. In May 1939 Merthyr Tydfil Corporation placed a contract for nine bodies on Bristol chassis. The work resulted in a busy time for Chief Draughtsman Alf Bramley and the drawing office team, because there were three types of body involved. Bristol K5G chassis were used for the double-deckers, five 56-seat highbridge and one 53-seat lowbridge. The other three were 36-seat rear-entrance bodies on Bristol L5G single-deck chassis.

The teak-framed bodies bore some similarities to those built for Newcastle, but there were significant differences, and the new designs clearly pointed the way towards the future post-war NCB double-deckers. Distinguishing features included the rounded outside corners at the top of the windows at the front of the upper deck, and the deep waist rails on both decks, and there was a family resemblance in the single-deckers. The lower decks and the single-deckers featured 'D' shaped end windows. What was to become a distinguishing NCB feature made its first appearance on the Merthyr double-deckers, this was the shape of the upper deck emergency window. The single pane of glass had straight parallel top and bottom edges, but the sides were tapered outwards from the top. This characteristic was already well established on London trolleybuses and Leyland double-deck bodies, but unlike them the bottom corners on the NCB version had sharp corners. Merthyr paid £650 each for the double-deck bodies and each single-decker cost £475. Delivered in autumn 1939, they were long lived, though like many pre-war buses, they were heavily rebuilt in later years. It is unfortunate that the war prevented sales of similar bodies to other operators.

An event that was probably significant to the rapid development of the company's bus output over the next few years was the appointment of a new sales manager in June 1939. The man given the job was John Angus; he came to NCB from a similar position with Massey Bros of Wigan. Prior to that, he had worked for the English Electric Co at their Preston coachbuilding facility. While the authors are well aware that bus bodies, like cars, follow fashion trends, it is intriguing to notice a number of similarities between the new NCB double-deckers for Merthyr and the latest 1939 designs from Massey. These included not only the 'D' shaped end windows in the lower deck, but also the tapered sides of the glass in the upper deck emergency window. However, the reason for any similarities must remain a subject of conjecture, as Angus arrived after the Merthyr order had already been placed.

Only around 15 bus and coach bodies a year had been built since the inception of the company when the end of peacetime bus and coach production was marked by the delivery of FHN 757/8, two more Leyland Tiger TS8s, to Darlington Triumph in 1940. They were similar in many respects to the previous batch, but in addition to the slight step of the waistrail at the back, the main waistrail also featured a gentle curve.

Commercial vehicle construction also came to an end. Cattle truck and horse box construction was consigned to history, and commercial vehicles could only be built in accordance with a system of permits, which effectively rationed their supply to those who could demonstrate a need for a vehicle to support the war effort. Northern Coachbuilders was not involved in this, the Ministry of Supply had determined a different direction for the company.

Facing page, upper: The hand that designed the post-war **NCB** double-deckers can be seen clearly in this view of Merthyr Tydfil 28 (HB 5876), one of five 1939 highbridge bodies on Bristol K5G chassis. The symmetry of the semi-circular shaped lower deck 'D' windows is spoiled slightly by the addition of rain-shields whilst the use of coach-style side flashes is interesting. The teak-framed bodies were to a completely new design, differing from the Newcastle buses in many ways. This is the highbridge version, and the taper-sided emergency exit window can be seen.
(James Riddell)

Facing page, lower: The similarity with then-current **Massey** designs, as here for Kingston upon Hull, cannot have been a coincidence.
(Senior Transport Archive)

The 35-seat Darlington Triumph vehicles were of a versatile design, for use not only on lengthy stage carriage services, but also coach operation and private hire. The Triumph/NCB design of 1938-40 had evolved into a smoothly finished creation with shapely pillar surrounds, similar to other contemporary designs. After NCB had completed building eight of these bodies on Leyland Tiger TS8 chassis, war intervened; following which Triumph built their own bodies to a very similar design, mounted on Guy Arab chassis. Shown here is No. 56 (EHN 656) in the distinctive scarlet, orange and cream Triumph livery. *(James Riddell)*

47

The first **NCB** lowbridge body was built for Merthyr Tydfil. The application of a side-flash differently shaped to that of the highbridge version is interesting. (*James Riddell*)

There was a family resemblance also in the single-deckers, shown here by **HB 5881**. They shared with the double-deckers the 'D' shaped end windows. The Merthyr Tydfil single-deckers were to a new design, with little resemblance to any **NCB** single-deckers built previously but perhaps influenced by a demonstration vehicle which had visited Merthyr the previous year. (*James Riddell*)

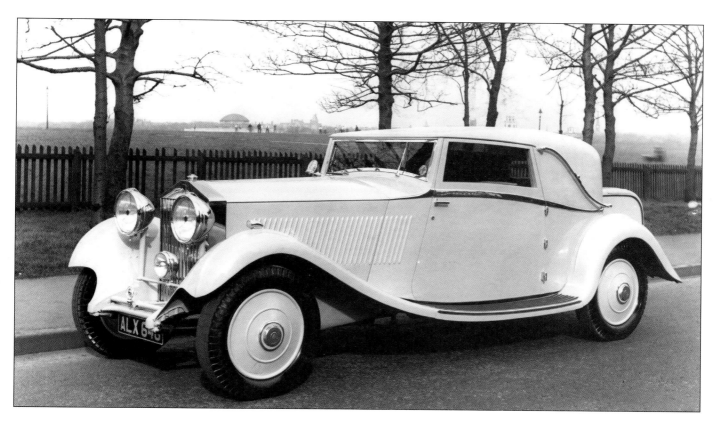

As the body of this 1934 Rolls Royce 20/25hp, ALX 646, is known to be by Barker, this stylish car must have come into Claremont Road for possible accident damage or repainting. It is not known to have Newcastle connections and the first owner had South African interests. The chassis number is only eight away from Sam Smith's saloon seen on page 22. ALX 646 was in the USA for a number of years but recently returned to the UK. *(K Price collection)*

This Rolls-Royce hearse was one of the more unusual jobs turned out by **NCB** craftsmen. The chassis, **XW 6652** was a Rolls-Royce Silver Ghost new in 1924, having probably served its time with the London carriage trade. Part of the original Hooper body was removed and replaced with this ornate hearse from a horse-drawn carriage. What a way to go! The 1930s NCB output included the repair and repaint of fine quality cars such as Rolls Royce and Bentley. *(James Riddell)*

5 – Mobilisation

War, and New Projects

Great Britain declared war on Nazi Germany on 3rd September 1939 and, as a precaution against air raids, the white concrete canopy at the front of the factory was given an elaborate pattern of camouflage paint. On 16th September petrol rationing for private cars was introduced, and bus and coach operators were only allocated a fraction of the fuel previously used by them. Consequently, many car users were now using the reduced bus services, so that standing loads became frequent. The last buses had to leave town and city centres by 10.00pm and Sunday services did not begin until mid-day in many places.

Northern Coachbuilders now found itself in the busiest period of its history. The desperate need for aircraft and military vehicles led to profound changes in the company output. One of the first orders received after hostilities began was for 39 breakdown tenders for the Royal Air Force, consisting of a platform and cab mounted on Crossley type IGL3 three-axle military chassis.

The amount of work anticipated was going to be greater than could be handled at Claremont Road, and late in 1939 a former airship hangar some nine miles away at Cramlington in Northumberland was leased to the company by the Ministry of War Transport. This 44,000 sq ft corrugated iron building was ideal for the production of large structures such as aircraft tails and double-deck buses, but this also meant that it was almost impossible to heat it during the winter months. The coke stoves proved quite inadequate for the task, and rain and snow found their way through the badly fitting panels, driven by the north east gales. However, it was not until 1943 that the whole of this building came into use.

Mass small car production almost came to a standstill, but numbers of new larger models such as the Ford V8 and Austin, Morris & Humber 18 and 20hp cars arrived at Claremont Road to be converted for wartime use. After all extraneous bodywork had been cut away, they were fitted with bodies for use as ambulances, mobile canteens, field surgeries, first aid centres and even libraries. Nearly all were painted grey or khaki and the various sets of

One of the first wartime contracts fulfilled by NCB was for a batch of tenders for the RAF based on the 6x4 version of the Crossley IGL3 (Indian Government Lorry 3ton). Many thousands of Crossleys were built during the war, and NCB received a share of the work to equip them for the conflict. *(James Riddell)*

A miscellany of vehicles lined up outside the newly completed west extension of the factory in 1939 and standing in Wallace Street; please see page 26 for a plan of the factory. Next to the flatbed lorry for Geo Lockney & Sons is the familiar Ringtons Tea horse-drawn van, clearly brought out for the occasion, but then a Domestos van also making the connection with financially associated firms as mentioned in the text. At the far end the United Automobile company's vans can be made out. This would be amongst the last, or perhaps *the* last time such a line up of vehicles for local and other traders would be possible before wartime priorities took precedence. *(James Riddell)*

I am the Glider...

I am the silent aircraft that takes those intrepid airborne troops stealthily into action behind the enemy's lines. When the continent of Europe is being invaded, I shall be in front of the Second Front!

I am made by the Motor Industry, whose collaboration with the Aircraft Industry is functioning with the precision of a fine machine. This conjoint effort is an outstanding example of the initiative and driving force of Free Enterprise.

When Victory is won, both industries will make a major contribution to winning the Peace. Both will subscribe in great measure to the Government's policy for full employment.

THE MOTOR INDUSTRY
Production for Victory

In 1944 a series of advertisements was produced illustrating some of the work done by the motor industry for the war effort. This one shows a Hamilcar glider; the tails for many of these monsters were built at Cramlington by NCB. *(Geoff Burrows collection)*

recognition letters, such as ARP (Air Raid Precautions), NFS (National Fire Service), NAAFI (Navy, Army, & Air Force Institute), WVS (Women's Voluntary Service) and MOI (Ministry of Information) became familiar sights on the completed vehicles. One example was an urgent order for 101 mobile canteens for the NAAFI that was built by NCB in 1940.

In addition to this type of work, parts of the factory were gradually turned over to aircraft production. This was similar in many ways to bus and coach work, and some valuable lessons were learnt which were useful after the war ended. Amongst the items produced were the hinged trailing edges for Barracuda wings, and fuselage and cockpit areas for Hawker Typhoon and Tornado fighter aircraft. Over two million aircraft components and small pieces were made for aircraft including the Hamilcar Glider, Lancaster, Barracuda, Swordfish, Mosquito, Grumman Martlet and Blackburn Botha.

The work was not restricted to wheeled vehicles; for example 13,000 ammunition crates were supplied. When Britain sent aid to Murmansk in Russia with the 'Arctic Convoys' following Hitler's invasion of the Soviet Union in September 1941, it included tanks and guns built on Tyneside at the giant Vickers-Armstrong works. Employees at NCB worked day and night for weeks building boxes and covers as protection for the armaments on board ship on their journey to that besieged country. Another product was a specially shaped cover for the 25 pound guns sent to the war zones overseas. Many thousands of these 'gun cosies' were manufactured from camouflage netting, to conceal the weapons when not in use.

In order to focus British industry on the manufacture of armaments, on 20th July 1940 the Government stopped the production of all non-essential goods, including buses. To buy or sell a bus new or otherwise, it was necessary to obtain a licence from the local Regional Transport Commissioner. The petrol ration for private motoring was withdrawn, and motorists were advised to remove the batteries and rotor arms, and jack their cars up onto wood blocks in their garages 'for the duration'. Many bus operators were soon in a very difficult situation, because they were being asked to carry more passengers than ever before, and thousands of extra journeys were being made by people engaged

The gas-bag framework on this South Shields Daimler was constructed by NCB. Shortly after this photograph, taken in the market-place, all the buildings shown were demolished by Nazi bombers. *(Newcastle Journal)*

With the outbreak of WWII, most private motoring had to cease and many large cars were used for community or military purposes. Sam Smith's Rolls Royce (page 22) has now been rebodied as an ambulance for St John, registered in Northumberland in July 1939, and is seen in Claremont Road in wartime trim with white bumper and headlamp masks. *(James Riddell)*

In addition to new vehicles, numbers of both new and used cars were requisitioned for war work. This line-up of 18 and 20hp Austins for the **YMCA** shows three 'tea cars' and two mobile libraries that **NCB** converted by removing the major part of the bodywork. The nearest car is a 1937 model, whereas the second and fifth were new in 1934. The centre car is curious in that its registration, EUP 882, is mid-1942 (EUP 881 was a Stockton Corporation Leyland TD7 bus!), implying that the car had either not been previously registered, or had lost the original number. Note that some nearside headlamps are masked, and some offside, as there was no specific regulation at this time. *(James Riddell)*

This line-up of Humber 18s and Ford V8s was part of an urgent order for mobile canteens ready for collection in Claremont Road in 1940. Instead of luxury saloon bodies, they were fitted out as refreshment vans for the **NAAFI**. *(James Riddell)*

on essential war work to factories that could only be reached by bus. Fuel was severely rationed, and the Ministry of War Transport had requisitioned many buses and coaches, without leave of appeal.

Liquid fuel of any kind was desperately short, as it was all imported by ship, and these were being sunk every day by German U-boats. Many experiments were made to find ways to use alternative fuels, including creosote, town gas and producer gas, the latter made by heating anthracite (a very high quality coal) or coke in specially constructed trailers. An interesting order was received from South Shields Corporation in June 1940, to build a roof-mounted frame to house a gas bag on a single-deck Daimler bus. The bus became the subject of much speculation in that town, because it ran without the gas bag until the equipment to convert the diesel engine to town gas operation was manufactured. The most popular story was that the population was about to be evacuated, and the roof frame was for the carriage of luggage!

Most bus operators soon found that they had too few buses, and the extra mileage was wearing them out very quickly. Eventually the Government was persuaded to relent, and the first move was to release the vehicle production that had been 'frozen' in 1940. The total came to just over 400 chassis to serve the whole United Kingdom. There were even fewer bodies available for completion to be mounted on these chassis, about 130, and action to rectify this deficit was urgently needed.

The official drawing for the highbridge wartime vehicle. Note that at this stage a Leyland chassis was anticipated and the first example, supplied to London Transport, was indeed on a Titan TD7 chassis. *(Senior Transport Archive)*

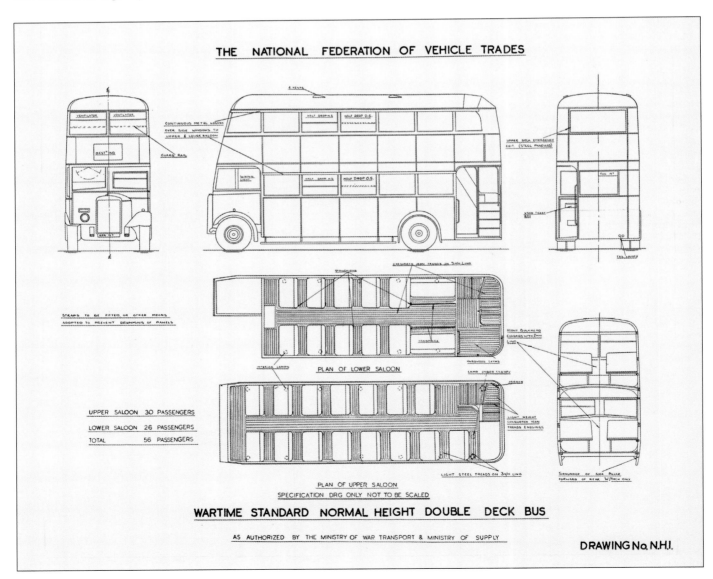

THE NATIONAL FEDERATION OF VEHICLE TRADES

UPPER SALOON 30 PASSENGERS
LOWER SALOON 26 PASSENGERS
TOTAL 56 PASSENGERS

PLAN OF LOWER SALOON

PLAN OF UPPER SALOON
SPECIFICATION DRG ONLY NOT TO BE SCALED

WARTIME STANDARD NORMAL HEIGHT DOUBLE DECK BUS

AS AUTHORIZED BY THE MINISTRY OF WAR TRANSPORT & MINISTRY OF SUPPLY

DRAWING No. N.H.I.

The National Federation of Vehicle Trades and Operators Joint Technical and Advisory Committee was set up to agree the specifications for wartime bodies that could be built using the minimum of material and labour. The manufacturers were given the details of the specifications for the highly standardised highbridge and lowbridge double-deck and single-deck bodies in July 1941, and the age of the 'utility' bus had begun. The first of these bodies would be built for the 'unfrozen' chassis, and Northern Coachbuilders was one of the firms authorised by the Ministry of Supply to build them.

The paperwork was very quickly turned into hardware, because the first NCB utility bus was completed in November 1941. This was a lowbridge-bodied Leyland TD7 for Leigh Corporation, and it was quickly followed by five more TD7s for highbridge bodies, two for Sheffield and one each for Birmingham, Western SMT and Young's of Paisley. Early in 1942 seven AEC Regent chassis arrived, of these four were allocated lowbridge bodies, two for Barton of Nottingham and two for Western Welsh. The latter also received two of the highbridge version, and the Mansfield bus operator Ebor received one.

In December 1941, the general manager of the Leigh undertaking reported that he had been allocated the first wartime Leyland buses, and while he may only have been referring to his six chassis, it is known that one of these, No. 84

This 'unfrozen' Leyland Titan TD7 of 1942 carried the only NCB body built for Birmingham Corporation. It is seen in original form with grey paint, no emergency window glass and only one half-drop opening window on each side of each deck. These no doubt proved quite ineffective in removing cigarette fumes, and most later bodies were given hopper ventilators in the upper deck front windows. Perry Bar garage was home to 1328 (FON 328), but TD7s had short lives and this one was no exception, being withdrawn and scrapped after only seven years. (David Harvey collection)

Following a post-war repaint, the same Leyland became easily recognisable as a Birmingham bus. (David Harvey collection)

55

56

(FTB 11) carried the first NCB utility body. Of even more interest to the readers of this book is the fact that this bus still exists in preservation.

The man now in charge of all this activity was Production Director Richard Booth. He was well known in the industry, having come from Weymann's of Addlestone in Surrey. His presence may have assisted NCB in gaining entry into the national coachbuilding scene.

The Ministry of Supply then sanctioned the production of a limited number of new chassis, also to a wartime specification, and listed the coachbuilders who would be allowed to build the bodies. NCB was not one of these, instead the firm was directed to build new utility replacement bodies on old chassis. Major body repairs were not to be undertaken. Letters confirming this were received from the Vehicle Maintenance and Repair Division of the Ministry of Supply in September 1943, but these would appear to have been merely verification of the authority, as a number of bodies had already been built. It should be noted that operators had no choice regarding the make of body allocated to them. To maximise the number of passengers carried, it was also agreed that some single-deck buses could be re-bodied as double-deckers, and this was later to result in an interesting conversion.

As will be seen from the photographs, the wartime NCB body was uncompromising and severe in design. It was not adapted from pre-war designs, and met the utility specification completely. Composite construction method was used, but no aluminium was available, and all the exterior panels were of mild steel. Windows were fitted by the system known as 'direct' glazing, with a 'U' shaped rubber fitted round the glass, which was then held in position by wood fillets. No interior panels were fitted, except for the lower deck ceiling, but the structures were sound, and at first the timber used was well seasoned and quite suitable for the job. Unfortunately, this situation did not last long, as supplies soon ran out.

Though the specification of the utility buses had been decided by a committee, each manufacturer had its own interpretation of it. Thus, with

One of the early utility **NCB** bodies, Sheffield 477 (HWA 277) was built on this Leyland **TD7** chassis. As with all the **NCB** bodies on 'unfrozen' chassis, it did not feature opening ventilators at the front of the top deck. *(Keith Beedon)*

careful observation, it was possible to identify the coachbuilder by one or two distinguishing features. For example, on the NCB body the rearmost window on the side of upper deck had vertical sides, but the upper edge sloped down slightly towards the back.

No window in the upper deck emergency door was allowed on the early utility bodies. Passengers and conductors alike protested vigorously at this, because they could not see the stairs, a number of passengers were reported to have fallen, and it was difficult to see where you were. The Ministry relented after a few months and allowed the fitting of the window. Many operators themselves replaced the blank panel with a window at a later date. Then came a more painful imposition, wooden slatted seats. Fortunately, NCB was not greatly affected by this, because in most cases the seats from the old bodies were available for re-use, after being given attention by the trimming department. It was also found to be possible to make new seats even when the old ones were unsuitable. These were of simple wood and steel angle construction, neatly trimmed in whatever material happened to be available.

The emergency window in the upper deck was, in most wartime NCB bodies, a full height square shape divided vertically in the middle. In some the glass was the same width, but reduced in height, producing two equal sized squares. The bodies on the unfrozen chassis had plain front upper deck windows, but most of the re-bodied buses had hinged glass ventilators at the top. Opening windows were restricted to one on each side of each deck, and the rear registration number was painted onto the back platform window.

As the old buses began to arrive in some numbers, a systematic approach was given to the work of fitting the new bodies. It was realised that there would be a mixture of chassis types, and the design was arranged to accommodate these. To suit the new standard designs and to speed up the work, jigs were constructed to build the body units ready for assembly. The main body underframes had to be individually built, because the position and size of such things as floor traps to gain access to the mechanical components underneath varied on almost every job.

The production of the NCB replacement bodies for old chassis began in early 1943. Many of the earliest of these were on the short 25ft 0in chassis versions, but in 1932 the maximum overall length for double-deckers had been increased to 26ft 0in. Varying the length of the rearmost main side windows accommodated the differences in length and wheelbase on NCB bodies.

Because Ringtons core business of selling tea was severely curtailed by the Government at this time, the company was prohibited from operating the door-to-door motor van deliveries. The anticipated NCB output would now have to provide the majority of the group income, but little capital was available to finance this activity. NCB was wholly owned by Ringtons, which was forced to involve Lloyds Bank who took a debenture in the firm and provided the money needed. This was only achieved after Sam Smith gave his personal guarantee to the bank, in order to keep the company alive. The debenture was finally redeemed in 1954.

All the utility bus production was moved to Cramlington, together with the jigs and fixtures used for their sub-assemblies and main assemblies. The Claremont Road factory supplied Cramlington with the output from the woodmill, blacksmiths shop and trim shop (upholstery), as these facilities were not moved. For much of the remainder of the war, Claremont Road produced aircraft components and sub assemblies. The largest of these were the wings for the huge Hamilcar gliders, used to transport troops for the D-Day and Arnhem airborne landings. The tails for these monsters were built in the lofty hanger at Cramlington.

Five production lines were set up at Cramlington. Two were dedicated to the production of the utility buses, while the other three lines were busy with other types of work for the armed forces and emergency services. A small drawing office was also established there, under Alf Bramley, who had come from the Claremont Road office.

To enable the skilled staff and management to get to Cramlington, Armstrong's of Westerhope, using two former Glasgow Corporation double-deck Leyland buses with open staircases, operated a bus service from Newcastle for the company. They were a far cry from the luxurious buses and coaches formerly built by NCB. In addition, quite a number of people were recruited locally, and went on to make their careers in the coachbuilding industry. The company also rented additional premises in the Quayside area of Newcastle to build military vehicle bodies. Other sites used, where essential maintenance and repair work on small vehicles was also undertaken, were at City Road in Newcastle and Sunderland Road, Gateshead. The number of employees at the NCB factories reached a peak of 1,350 during the war.

The local British Electric Traction group (BET) operator, Northern General Transport, was amongst the first customers to receive an allocation of NCB bodies. This was the beginning of a business relationship that existed until the end of production at NCB. All the wartime replacement bodies for Northern were highbridge versions, built on AEC Regent chassis.

The Tyneside Tramways & Tramroads Co Ltd was an independent concern in 1931 when it bought a batch of Leyland TD1s, but became part of the Northern General group in 1936. The Leyland bodies required replacement during the war, and the utility NCB highbridge body of No. 8 (TY 7913) in the attractive Tyneside green and cream livery is seen in the Haymarket, Newcastle in June 1950. (Alan Cross)

Bomb damaged buses began to make their way to NCB for new bodies. Grimsby sent two AECs (JV 4694/5), and a Regent and a Leyland Titan TD5 came from Great Yarmouth (EX 3691 and EX 5010) respectively. The Essex operators Benfleet & District and Canvey & District both sent AEC Regents to NCB for replacement bodies. Benfleet owned two former Wallasey Corporation double-deckers (HF 7435/7), and Canvey operated a similar bus originally in the South Wales fleet (WN 4761), and a former Eastern National bus (VX 4108). More old AECs for new bodies came from Bournemouth (LJ 5802/5, TR 9454-6), the latter three had originated with Southampton Corporation. Highbridge bodies were fitted to all these AECs; another Essex independent, Moore Bros of Kelvedon, was the operator of a new lowbridge utility NCB body, on a former City of Oxford AEC Regent (WL 9068).

Leylands formed the largest marque of chassis to be re-bodied by NCB during the war, and the authors have identified 85. The oldest chassis dated from 1928, and it says much for the reliability of Leylands that their owners wished to keep them in service for as long as possible. Once again, the pre-1932 TD1 chassis received the 25ft 0in 'short bay' bodies. From 1932 the Leyland Titan TD2 and succeeding models were 26ft 0in long, and examples of all except the TD6 type were to receive NCB utility bodies.

At the beginning of the war, several bus fleets had been rapidly enlarged with large numbers of second-hand buses, to serve the 'shadow' factories set up by the Government to produce armaments. There were also aerodromes and military camps to be built and served by civilian workers; inevitably these were in country areas not previously served by buses other than occasional market day services. Many of these buses were time expired but for the war and would have been scrapped, but instead they were re-bodied for a second lease of life.

Prominent in the list of fleets called upon for these extra duties were Cumberland, Ribble and Wilts & Dorset Motor Services. They all sent buses to NCB for new bodies. Cumberland bought 15 lowbridge bodies for Leyland TD1s, TD2s and a TD7, for which they paid £1,165 each. Wilts & Dorset took seven on TD1s, and Ribble Motor Services modernised its own fleet of TD1s with six similar lowbridge bodies in 1943. The same type of body was supplied to Hebble Motor Services (four TD4s), South Wales (two TD5s), Hicks of Braintree Essex (one TD1), Griffin of Brynmawr in Wales (one TD2) and Wigan Corporation (one TD7). The Wigan bus (JP 4707) had an unfortunate history. New in 1940, it was not a year old before a bomb damaged the Leyland lowbridge body. Wigan sent it to RY Pickering in Wishaw, Lanarkshire, where it was rebuilt in 1941. Once again it became a casualty of the war when the body was totally wrecked, following which it was sent to NCB for a new body in 1943. This time it survived, and was sold for further service after the war.

An independent operator who had bought a number of buses to transport war workers sent six of them to NCB for new bodies. Formerly a coach operator, Kearsey's of Cheltenham had built up a fleet of double-deckers in 1939 when it gained contracts to carry employees of the Gloucester Aircraft Company to their factories. In 1943 four former Bolton Corporation Leyland TD1s and two ex-City of Oxford Motor Services AEC Regents were given new NCB utility highbridge bodies.

Highbridge bodies were produced in some numbers for Leyland chassis. Another of the associated Northern General companies, the Tyneside Tramways & Tramroads Company, took four on TD1s and one on a TD3. Rawtenstall Corporation had two TD3s, and TD4s were re-bodied for Devon General (four) and a TD5 for West Riding. The only NCB utility body for United was built on a TD2. Stockton Corporation received two on TD5 chassis in 1945, after some involved discussions between the manager, his committee and NCB.

There were also some unusual versions. Scout Motor Services, Preston converted two Leyland TS6 single-deck chassis to double-deck for lowbridge bodies. Similarly, Harper Bros of Heath Hayes in Staffordshire modified a single-deck Leyland TS3 chassis to take a standard utility highbridge body. After the war had ended, the chassis was scrapped and the body was fitted to a wartime Guy Arab chassis bought from Sheffield Corporation.

Another oddment was created from a single-deck Leyland Lion LT5A chassis for Leon Motor Services of Finningley, near Doncaster. Leon wished to put a double-deck body on the chassis, but lacked the resources of the larger operators, so the end of the chassis was cut off to shorten it to the required length of 26ft 0in. There was then no room left to place the normal rear-entrance platform behind the rear axle. To get around the problem Northern Coachbuilders built a new 55-seat body with a central entrance and staircase! The authors believe that only one other similar body was built during the war, by Birch Brothers, also on a Leyland Lion for their own fleet.

The only Daimler bus chassis to receive an NCB utility body had been a fire victim. New to Caerphilly Urban District Council in 1944, it was a type CWA6 with a utility lowbridge Duple body. A depot fire in April of that year destroyed several buses in the fleet, and damaged FNY 515. The bus was sold to the Swan Motor Co of Swansea, where eyewitnesses report that it did not appear to be badly damaged. However, Swan scrapped the body and sent the chassis to NCB, where it received a new utility highbridge body.

Wherever possible women were employed to release men for the armed forces, and it was quickly found that these women could fulfil many tasks normally given to men. 'The girls' built products such as ammunition boxes and bus seats, but they were soon entrusted with work on the utility buses. As a propaganda feature, in 1943 a double-deck bus body was constructed

Of all the Northern General group wartime bodies, that built on 25ft 0in long 1932 AEC Regent 562 (CN 5240) had the greatest claim to fame. Built at Cramlington, it was paraded before the transport press at Claremont Road in April 1944. Why? The body was built entirely by female labour under the direction of foreman George Dobson, and the firm gained considerable publicity at the time. The comfortable seats from the old body were re-trimmed and fitted, but the destination display was minimal. Features such as headlamps had not been replaced when the photograph was taken. (JH Herdman collection)

entirely by a team of women. It was fitted to Northern General AEC Regent No. 562 (CN 5240), that had been new in 1932 with a petrol engine and a Short Bros body.

Officially, Northern Coachbuilders was not on the list of approved builders of single-deck replacement bodies, but at least two are known to have been constructed, presumably because of the location of their owners. Venture Transport of Consett, in the west of County Durham, owned a number of Maudslay SF40 buses. These vehicles had an unusual layout for the time, the driver sat alongside the engine, which was mounted in the centre, ahead of the front axle. This allowed the entrance to be situated to the nearside of the engine at the front, leaving enough space inside the bus for 40 seats. One of these buses (BPT 789) was severely damaged in an accident following total

Throughout the country women were recruited to replace men serving in the forces, as recorded in the text, and here we see some of the **NCB 'girls'** busy working on the framing for double-decker bus bodies at Cramlington in 1943. *(JH Herdman collection)*

brake failure, fortunately without any loss of life or severe injuries. In 1943 it was sent to NCB where a new body of utility design was built for it. At about the same time Darlington Triumph sent one of their 1937 TSM coaches (DHN 102) that had also sustained severe damage to the NCB body. This vehicle was also fitted with a new NCB utility body.

As well as replacing old bodies with new utility bodies, and despite the original Ministry ruling, NCB carried out heavy repair work on older buses where new bodies could not be justified. Examples of double-deckers so treated include four English Electric-bodied AECs belonging to Bournemouth Corporation (LJ 5800/1/3/4) re-conditioned in 1944, and Wakefield's Motors FT 2609, also an AEC. Wakefield's was another Northern General subsidiary, operated as part of the Tynemouth fleet. Two accident damaged Manchester Corporation Crossley Mancunian buses were repaired in 1946. The Crossley body on 513 (AXJ 980), new in 1935 and the body on 726 (EVR 350), built in Manchester Corporation's own workshops in 1938, were both constructed on MCCW steel framework.

A few single-deck buses were similarly treated. Several local operators had buses and coaches requisitioned at the beginning of the war, and when they were returned to their owners some considerable amounts of work were often required to bring them back to roadworthy condition. NCB would appear to have shared some of this work, which included four Northern side-engined SE6 class single-deck buses.

The amount and variety of work produced by NCB during the war years was considerable. In addition to the vehicles mentioned earlier, the Royal Air Force was supplied with 94 Crossley IGL3 chassis fitted with crates for the transport of gas cylinders for barrage balloons, complete with two-axle trailers. Another 167 Crossley chassis, this time the two-axle FWD, were equipped

A fascinating 1945 view of part of the interior of the Cramlington factory. Its previous use as an airship hangar explains the vast size and tremendous height. Since it would be impossible to heat the space it begs the question how did they provide any form of heating for those employed in this cavernous construction? Is the answer to be seen in the bottom right hand corner of the picture? Vehicles in build include two for Bolton (see page 168) with their distinctive destination layout arrangement and painted into normal fleet livery. They would have an interesting life, being transferred by the operator to somewhat newer chassis a few years later. Completed body sections can be seen stacked against the wall and also in the centre of the photograph. The appurtenances of the panel workers are clear to see in the foreground whilst behind the completed vehicle the framing of a top deck can be seen under construction. The glass-windowed wall enclosed the paint shop behind which can be seen the Commer and Morris-Commercial company lorries. *(James Riddell)*

Cumberland Motor Services built up a large fleet of early-model Leyland Titans during the war, to serve the military camps and shadow factories that sprang up in the area. This Leyland TD2 was new to Summerskill of Twickenham, with a Birch highbridge body. London Passenger Transport Board acquired it in November 1933 numbering it L88 before reclassifying it TD37. It was sold to dealer Norths in March 1940, and snapped up immediately by Cumberland where it became number 156. In September 1943 the body was replaced with this NCB 53-seat lowbridge utility example and a Gardner 5LW engine replaced the former petrol unit. *(SL Poole)*

Bournemouth 61 (TR 9456) was one of four AEC double-deckers bought from Southampton in 1938. New in 1930, the original Park Royal bodies were replaced by single-deck Beadle examples removed from scrapped Thornycroft chassis in 1940. Finally in September 1944 they were returned to double-deck status with new utility NCB bodies. *(Alan Cross)*

Above: Many Grimsby Corporation buses suffered badly during the wartime air raids. AEC Regent 55 (JV 4964) was one of several rebodied by NCB in 1945. It remained in service long enough to become part of the Grimsby-Cleethorpes fleet when the two operators merged in 1957, retaining the same fleet number. Here it is inside Victoria Road North garage in the Grimsby-Cleethorpes livery. It remained in use until withdrawn in 1962. *(Michael Dryhurst)*

Below: New to the Miller Traction Co in 1932, this Leyland Titan TD2 passed to London Transport before being sold to Griffin of Brynmawr, south Wales. It was one of several Griffin were authorised to send to NCB for new bodies in 1943. This depot view shows the classic recognition features of the wartime NCB body, the two upright emergency windows and the almost rectangular upper deck rear side windows. The two per side half-drop opening windows remain in place as built. *(Alan Cross)*

with wireless transmitter van bodies. Numbers of Albion chassis passed down the production lines fitted with mobile workshop bodies. Another 100 Albions were supplied with steel general-purpose lorry bodies. Just how many trailers of various kinds were built is not possible to determine; of those known, there were 100 low-loaders for the transport of aircraft, and 198 searchlight trailers. To provide refreshments for service personnel working out in the open on the many airfields, 'coffee' trailers were constructed.

Another contract required the construction of 400 army scout cars. The Ford V8 chassis for these were delivered to Claremont Road, before being driven to Cramlington, where their bodies were built. After completion, they were driven back to Newcastle motor dealers Murray & Charlton Ltd , to await collection by the military authorities.

As the war progressed, so the needs of the armed forces developed. Mobile radar cabins on Austin and Crossley three-axle chassis required a production line to themselves. Known at first as 'RDF' until it was given the appellation of 'radar' by the Americans, this was then a top-secret project. It has been said that the army advanced across Europe so quickly after 'D-day' that the radar units, meant to give warning of air attacks, never caught up!

To serve the religious needs of the armed forces, two mobile churches were built, following the designs of similar units built in the Middle East by the Royal Engineers. They were mounted on Commer chassis, and featured large doors at the back which opened out to make space for the congregation, whilst inside there was an altar and pulpit. They were also equipped with an early version of the 'sleeper cab', where the padre had his 'billet'. One of these was handed over at a civic ceremony outside St George's Cathedral in Newcastle. Another order called for four mobile libraries; we have no record of how the troops were supposed to return the books with the front line moving forward every day!

As was usual then, apprentices were trained alongside skilled men on these production lines. At the suggestion of the trade union, a training school was set up at Nelson village, close to Cramlington, for the youngest of these boys, aged between 14 and 16 years old. They were trained not only in the use of tools and measuring equipment, but to also recognise the different types of wood and metal, and the uses to which they could be put.

Leon, of Finningley, Yorkshire, owned a four-cylinder engined Leyland Lion LT5A (JP 42). So why did **NCB** fit a centre entrance highbridge body to it in 1944? Because the long wheelbase single-deck chassis precluded the fitment of the normal rear bulkhead and platform, this unique body was produced to solve the problem. It is as well that the roads in the area were flat, as progress in the fully laden bus would have been leisurely. This is the only picture that the authors could locate, taken after it was withdrawn, and with a boarded-up upper deck front window. *(R Holmes)*

The boxy wartime body probably looked its best on AEC Regent chassis, in this case an early short wheelbase model. The Essex operator Canvey & District owned VX 4108, photographed on Canvey Island in more rural days. The interior of the bus was even more spartan, with wooden seating and only two half-drop opening windows on each deck. *(Alan Cross)*

With the onset of war Wilts & Dorset Motor Services urgently needed extra double-deckers to serve military bases and 'shadow' factories built in rural areas. Numbers of elderly Leyland Titans were purchased, in this case former Southdown UF 7382, and the TD1 of 1931 was sent to NCB in 1944 for rebodying, while still petrol engined. By the time this photograph was taken the bus had acquired a Gardner 5LW engine, a 'Covrad' replacement radiator, and the lowbridge body had received improved ventilation with top sliding windows. Ironically, earlier in the war, Wilts & Dorset had sold six Leyland TD1s to Southdown! *(The Omnibus Society)*

The only wartime Daimler chassis to receive a utility NCB body was FNY 515 which had started life with Caerphilly UDC, where the original Duple body was damaged by fire. It was bought by Swan Motors of Swansea and sent to NCB for a new highbridge body. After the war Swan was acquired by United Welsh, in whose livery the Daimler CWA6 is seen, surrounded by Duple-bodied Albion coaches. *(CJ Taylor collection)*

In 1937 Stockton Corporation bought six Cravens-bodied Leyland TD5c buses. Rapid deterioration of the bodies led Stockton to seek permission for replacements. As a result, two were sent to NCB in 1945, where the full utility specification bodies were built. HV Burlingham of Blackpool rebodied the other four in 1946. *(RC Davis)*

Middlesbrough Exchange is the town centre terminus where Corporation 26 (XG 2327) is standing. This 1934 Leyland was one of six to receive a new relaxed NCB lowbridge body in 1945, but note the continued use of the rear angular dome. Only one of the batch had a rounded dome. *(Roy Marshall)*

One of Darlington Triumph's 1935 NCB bodied TSMs required a new body during the war. It was sent back to Newcastle, and received one of only two NCB single-deck utility bodies known to have been built. Shown in post-war days in the attractive fully lined out Triumph livery, DHN 102 is seen alongside another TSM in the fleet with the operator's own body, built in 1936 to the same style as those bodied by NCB. *(RC Davis)*

It was usual in those days for apprentices to be instructed alongside skilled men on the production lines. In a move to improve training, a school was started at Nelson village, close to the Cramlington factory, for the youngest apprentices, aged between 14 and 16 years old. A group of boys is seen here examining a scale model of a lower deck framework that they had constructed under the guidance of their instructor (third from the left). Unlike today's regime of health and safety laws, the only concession to working conditions was a pair of overalls.
(Geoff Burrows collection)

This Yorkshire Traction Leyland TD4 had started life with Hebble Motor Services in 1935. After transfer to 'Tracky' it was given a lowbridge NCB body in 1945. The ventilation was improved, but the vestigial destination display was unchanged despite the larger aperture now available. (Roy Marshall)

The first LPTB Guy Arab bus with an NCB utility body, G30 (GLF 680) is shown here leaving its garage to enter service, centre, and below on Wembley High Road. As related on page 71, it was built under the 'relaxed' utility regime, so had additional opening windows but retains the angular rear roof panels. (Alan Cross both)

6 – Pacification

Preparations for Peace

In 1944 the population, though tired and weakened by the war, began to realise that Hitler had lost his chance to defeat Great Britain, and sooner or later mainland Europe would be invaded by Allied troops. Thus, a quiet sense of confidence and hope began to emerge and manifested itself in the beginnings of post-war planning.

A new member joined the management team in 1944. Horace Hatton had been General Manager of Brush Coachworks Ltd, of Loughborough, Leicestershire. He had a wealth of design experience behind him, and his appointment as Chief Engineer at NCB was timely. New design and drawing offices were built on a mezzanine floor at Claremont Road, and the wartime design staff from Cramlington moved there. Chief Draughtsman Alf Bramley and his team soon had plenty of work to do.

As soon as the 'second front' had been successfully created following the 'D-day' landings, the pressure for military work began to ease, and three of the Cramlington production lines could now be used for bus bodybuilding. The Ministry of Supply relaxed the utility specifications for bus builders from the end of the year. This relaxation allowed, amongst other things, the use of upholstered seats, aluminium panels instead of steel, more opening windows and curved panels for the rear domes in place of the angular wartime shapes. The improvements promised were only introduced gradually and slowly at NCB, and it was late in 1945 before any changes were apparent. The result was often a mix of full and relaxed utility versions going out at the same time.

Middlesbrough Corporation sent a batch of lowbridge buses for new bodies during 1945. The five Leyland TD3s carried the original version of the Leyland 'V-front' 'all-metal' body that had been the cause of much anguish because of the many faults in the design. Indeed, one of the drivers who collected the buses from Middlesbrough recalled that the low gangway projected a short distance through the driver's bulkhead. When he braked hard, the body moved so much that the gangway came forward and hit him on the back of the head! When the re-bodied buses were returned to Middlesbrough, four had angular

Horace Hatton

The southern-most operator of NCB bodies was Devon General, and one of the four rebodied Leyland Titans was active on the 12 service in August 1952 when the lady in the background would have been in the height of fashion. This fleet was always well-kept and smart and the utility body looks at its best with the replacement (and chromed) driver's windscreen surround even giving a touch of distinction! It looks quite smart in this summer view in Torquay. (*Alan Cross*)

rear domes and one the relaxed curved version. However, they were all fitted with six top deck sliding opening windows, and four in the lower deck.

Sunderland District, another Northern General subsidiary, received a similarly mixed batch of highbridge bodies in the same period, on seven AEC Regent double-deckers, the order was not completed until 1946. Two received angular 'utility' domes, and the remainder had a curved 'relaxed' version. There was also a mix of two styles of upper deck emergency windows, some with long tall glass and the rest with the small square version. Like many vehicles rebodied by NCB, they were fitted with the seats from the old bodies, suitably re-trimmed and quite comfortable to ride on.

The body on one of London's first utility Guys was destroyed by a flying bomb near Waterloo Station in mid-1944. The bus had been new in 1942 with a body built by Park Royal, an old established and well respected London bus builder. London Transport would have preferred to obtain the replacement body from the same coachbuilder, but Park Royal was not at that time authorised to build bodies on other than new chassis. In July 1944 LPTB was allocated an NCB body, and the Guy chassis arrived at Cramlington in August 1944, where the new body was built. Delivered back to London in January 1945, G30 (GLF 680) was the only standard NCB utility London bus. G30 was supplied with slatted wood seats, and painted in the normal LPTB red and white livery.

Northern Coachbuilders was, as has already been stated, only authorised to build replacement bus bodies. While customers were still desperate, the situation was easing slightly because some preferred to wait for new vehicles, now that the end of the war was in sight. The large Ministry of War Transport contracts were now coming to an end, and NCB found itself with spare capacity. Some of that was about to be filled in an unexpected manner.

Park Royal was given authority to build more bodies on new Guy Arab chassis for London at the beginning of 1945, and with other outstanding orders this meant that they had more work than they could cope with. The Ministry of Supply was approached, and it was agreed that NCB could build a trial body, using a kit of parts supplied by Park Royal. The bus, G139 (GYE 83), was delivered to LPTB at the beginning of May 1945, and was indistinguishable from the Park Royal version. Authority was then given for the supply of a further 15 identical bodies, G140-149 and G151-153 were delivered during the beginning of June, while G194 and G195 completed the order on 5th July 1945. The origin of these buses caused a mystery in the past, due to the fact that Park Royal manufactured the kits of parts, and in doing so issued their own body numbers

The cartoonists in the transport press could be relied on to raise a smile. *(Senior Transport Archive)*

"It's 'abit! I ain't painted a bus for over five years!"

There is nothing in this photograph to indicate that it shows anything other than a standard Park Royal utility body in the LPTB fleet. It is hardly surprising that the origin remained a mystery for some time. Showing that they were built in the 'relaxed utility' era Guy Arab/NCB G148 (GYE 92), has a rounded rear dome and extra opening windows. As with all LPTB utility buses the post-war repaint into red and cream is topped off with a brown roof.
(J Lines collection)

with them. Such sub-contracting is not unknown in the industry, even today.

When delivered, the bodies constructed by NCB were easily recognised by their livery. The main panels were painted in a shade of milk chocolate, and the roofs were in dark red oxide. For relief, the window frames appeared in bright yellow ochre. Internally, the seats were trimmed with orange and brown patterned moquette, whereas Park Royal used brown leathercloth. Details such as these were, of course, dependent on the availability of materials in a period of extreme shortages. Following these, a further ten were ordered, and G196-205 were delivered during the second half of August.

The name of Northern Coachbuilders was prominent in Ministry of Supply and London Transport circles at that time, because concurrently with the building of the new bus bodies came a contract to replace or rebuild six bodies for Green Line coaches. This came about because in July 1944 a German flying bomb (V1) entered Elmers End garage horizontally and exploded. Nine vehicles were badly damaged, but by using spare bodies, three were put back into service fairly quickly. The other six, after receiving attention to chassis damage, were sent to Newcastle for repair. In the instances of two of the coaches, T514 (ELP 238) and T560 (ELP 284), so great was the damage that NCB virtually provided new bodies. The other four were effectively total rebuilds, as they had to be completely stripped down to undertake the repairs. The work was completed early in 1946. These vehicles were members of the famous Green Line 10T10 class of coaches, with AEC Regal chassis. The original bodies were built by London Transport at their Chiswick Works. They remained in service with the LPTB until 1953, when the new RF class of underfloor-engined coaches and buses replaced the whole fleet of London Transport single-deckers.

One other vehicle arrived at Cramlington from London in 1945, of their unusual 'Q' class. This was again an AEC single-decker, but with the engine mounted at the side under the floor between the wheels, in similar fashion to the Northern

A Park Royal-bodied AEC Q operating on the Green Line service to Hertford soon after delivery. It was one of these war damaged vehicles which NCB was expecting to rebody but in the event the chassis was returned to London Transport and eventually scrapped.
(Senior Transport Archive)

As related in the text, the London Transport garage at Elmers End was virtually destroyed by a flying bomb in 1944. Above can be seen all that remained of Green Line coach T514 (ELP 238) after it had been pulled out of the wreckage.

After T514 had been rebuilt by NCB in 1945 it spent several years in Green Line service before being demoted along with the rest of the class to bus use, following the arrival of the replacement RF class Green Line coaches in 1951/2. Seen below leaving Kingston-on-Thames *en route* for Staines in 1951, T514 was eventually withdrawn in 1953.
(Alan Cross both)

General 'SE4' and 'SE6' classes of bus. The Park Royal body of Q217 (DGX 223) had been completely destroyed, and it was hoped that NCB could build a suitable replacement. The chassis stood untouched for some time, though a kit of parts was made to use for the construction of a new body. For reasons unknown to the authors, the work was never started, and the chassis, together with the kit, was returned to London. It stood unused until written off by London Transport in March 1946.

An unusual 'one-off' was built during 1945. Wilts and Dorset sent a 1930 Leyland TD1 chassis (RU 9493) north to receive its second utility body. The first one, which had been built by Duple in 1942, was destroyed by fire in December 1944. The completed bus looked quite unlike any other previous or future NCB body. It was of an interim design combining utility features with ideas that would be used in the new post-war bodies. The most significant of these features were window pans incorporating 'Widney' patented rubber sections that were adopted for all the main glazing.

These were the last new utility bodies to be built by NCB, and apart from repair and rebuilding work, the last work undertaken in the 'airship shed' was a very prestigious contract for London Transport.

During 1944 the Ministry of War Transport gave permission for both Bradford Corporation and London Transport to order new bodies for old trolleybus chassis, and they were directed to NCB for some of this work. The London order was for 20 bodies on three-axle chassis that had been rebuilt following bombing, when the bodies had been destroyed. Furthermore, London Transport wanted the bodies to look similar to their later classes of trolleybuses introduced in 1940. To accomplish this, a visit to the Fulwell trolleybus depot in London was made by NCB engineers in October to assess their vehicles. Bradford required replacements for six time-expired English Electric bodies mounted on AEC two-axle chassis that had been built in 1934, the new bodies were to resemble as far as possible the old bodies in style and proportion. The interesting point so far as Northern Coachbuilders was concerned, was that the appearance of the old London and Bradford bodywork was very similar, because in 1934 English Electric had been involved with the design developments in both fleets. Therefore, NCB prepared new designs of trolleybus for the two operators. Both had much in common, apart from the length, of course.

The London trolleybuses were to almost the full pre-war standard and merged into the fleet imperceptibly. Window pans with modern rubber section glazing of neat appearance was employed, and shaped windows at the ends and front of the upper deck. Seats were only available for half the new bodies, upholstered in blue patterned moquette with sprung cushions and hair padded squabs. The remainder were fitted after their arrival back in London. The exterior sparkled with the famous LPTB red paint and gold fleetnames, and inside all the wood cappings were painted blue to complement the seat covering. They joined the original London United fleet of UCC-bodied trolleybuses, and their wartime Weymann bodies built on chassis whose bodies had been destroyed in the blitz, in being the only London trolleybus bodies of composite construction. Most of the NCB-bodied trolleybuses were returned to the West Ham and Bexleyheath depots where they had been based at the time of the bombings, and apart from two early withdrawals remained in service until those depots were converted to motor bus operation in 1959.

There were two makes of chassis involved in the London exercise, AEC and Leyland. These were further sub-divided by LPTB into five different classes; B2 and D2 were Leylands, and E1, E2 and E3 AECs. The two B2 chassis were originally of a special short length with 60-seat bodies for use in narrow south London streets in the Croydon, Woolwich and Bexleyheath areas. Before despatch to NCB the chassis were rebuilt to the normal 30ft 0in length for standard London trolleybuses using new frames from LPTB spares stock. The design chosen for the body closely resembled the 'N1' London trolleybus class, built by the Birmingham Railway Carriage and Wagon Works in 1939.

Wilts & Dorset 40 (RU 9493) was a 1930 Leyland Titan TD1 acquired from Hants & Dorset in 1939, sent to NCB in 1945 after its 1942 Duple utility body had been destroyed by fire. The resulting new body was quite unlike any other, partly because it was fitted with 'Widney' rubber mounted glazing as a prelude to its adoption for the post-war standard body. When photographed in Pewsey, Wiltshire in 1951 the bus had a Gardner 5LW diesel engine and a 'Covrad' replacement radiator. (Alan Cross)

Facing page: The six Bradford Corporation replacement bodies on AEC 661T chassis were required to follow the proportions of their original 1934 English Electric-built bodies. They could be regarded as a stage in the development of the post-war standard body, with deeper lower deck waist panels and a less curvaceous rear profile. The utility style direct rubber glazing and push-out front hopper ventilation windows gave a more severe appearance to these otherwise well-finished bodies. Here is No. 622 (AAK 424). Bradford's light blue livery has photographed well, contrasting with the camouflage paint clearly visible on the NCB brick and concrete frontage. See also page 180 for a further view of this vehicle.
(JH Herdman collection both)

Despite the variety of chassis types, all 20 of the NCB bodies were identical, and they retained their previous London fleet numbers, with the addition of 'C' suffix letters, to indicate that they had been rebodied by Northern Coachbuilders. The first was finished at Cramlington in November 1945; the rest were completed by August 1946.

This was an auspicious return of quality bus building for the company, and the largest order received to date. It was not achieved without difficulties, not the least being financial. The company had quoted a price based on the utility bodies then in production, having somewhat naively ignored the London specification. There were also other factors beyond their control; not only were materials and skilled labour in short supply but their cost, and wages, were escalating. LPTB eventually agreed a price for the bodies of almost 50% more than the original quotation. This situation was not unique, because East Lancashire Coachbuilders had obtained a similar contract for London Transport trolleybus bodies, and it too was forced to apply for an agreement to increase the price.

Northern Coachbuilders intended to capitalise on the London trolleybus contract, and issued several press advertisements showing pictures of the completed vehicles. Apparently London Transport took exception to this, and wrote to NCB reminding them that the bodies had been allocated by the Ministry of Supply, rather than chosen.

In a press statement at the end of the war, managing director Malcolm Smith confirmed that the company would not only be resuming bus bodybuilding, but intended to develop new specialities including caravans, paper board, glass fibre board and perambulators! The authors believe that the paper and glass fibre board would have been the prerogative of Cut-Out (Cartons) to manufacture, and that perhaps the press release had been misinterpreted. However, the company was seriously exploring the perambulator market, and the design department produced a papier-mâché prototype four-wheeled model. While none of these projects matured, NCB did commence manufacture of a new and successful product, described in the next chapter.

Standing outside St Luke's church in Claremont Road at the end of 1945 is the first of the London trolleybuses to be rebodied by NCB, 430C (DGY 430). The original MCCW body was destroyed by a VI 'Doodlebug' at West Ham depot. Note the camouflage on the factory canopy. *(James Riddell)*

London Transport trolleybus 385C (DGY 385) was one of 20 to receive new **NCB** bodies in 1945/6. This one is a Leyland reclassified as D2C, photographed after being placed outside the gates of the Newcastle Exhibition Park for the purpose. The quality of the work is apparent, despite the many problems that arose before the completion of the contract. The trolleys were fitted at the Fulwell works of London Transport after completion of the southward journey. *(JH Herdman collection)*

7 – Electrification

Battery-electric Vehicles

The company began a completely new venture in 1944. During the wartime fuel shortages, battery-electric vehicles had become very popular for local deliveries of milk and groceries, since petrol was not needed for them. The owners quickly became aware of the other merits of electric vehicles, economy and speed. For start-stop duties they were much faster than petrol vans, due to their superior acceleration, and the fact that the driver was freed from the time needed to operate a starter, clutch and gearbox. So much so that they were in great demand. Hatton had been responsible for much of the design of BEVs while at Brush. Thus, one of his first tasks at NCB was the design of a Northern Coachbuilders version.

Victory in Europe came in May 1945, just in time for the Farm Week Exhibition that took place in June on the Newcastle Town Moor. Prototypes of the new battery-electric vans were displayed on the company stand at the show. The first production vehicles, consisting of three-quarter and one ton vans and open milk floats, were built in a tiny garage near the Haymarket, Newcastle, as space was already at a premium in Claremont Road. Manufacture was moved to premises in Gateshead, on the Team Valley Trading Estate, during 1946. The 25,000 sq ft accommodation there consisted of a former works canteen in two large Nissen huts linked together by a brick built kitchen. One building was used to construct the chassis, the bodies and cabs were built in the other, and the former kitchen was used as offices and stores. Production was under

The first **NCB** battery-electric van to be built was photographed outside the factory as soon as it was completed, with the Managing Director Malcolm Smith on the right, and Horace Hatton, who designed it, at the front.
(Turner's [Photography] Ltd)

The prototype **NCB** 10/15cwt battery-electric van was built in 1946, and followed as closely as possible the design of a scale model made the previous year. Here it is being demonstrated at an agricultural show on Newcastle's Town Moor. Though it looked superb, it was much too ambitious to be produced at a competitive price, and remained unique. The central headlamp was also more decorative than practical. The production vehicles that followed were to a simpler, more practical design. *(Geoff Burrows collection)*

This Maidstone Co-op bakery van is a typical production version of the three-quarter ton **NCB** battery-electric van. *(Turner's [Photography] Ltd)*

Much ingenuity was shown by users of NCB electrics by finding different roles for them. West Cornforth Co-op bought this 14cwt milk float and fitted it out as a mobile greengrocery shop in 1948. A housewife is being served with her order in this posed scene. Note that polished bumpers have been added, improving the appearance as well as having a practical value. *(Turner's [Photography] Ltd)*

This BEV body design was specially prepared by NCB engineer Ken Challoner for use as a 14cwt company service van in 1948, working from premises behind Northumberland Street in the centre of Newcastle. The pressed steel car wheels have now been replaced by a heavy-duty commercial type, and the single headlamp has been moved to the nearside, in the light of practical experience. The externally placed sidelamps were found to be prone to damage, and have been flush mounted on the front panel. This special model was the only one with the driver's door hinged at the back. *(Turner's [Photography] Ltd)*

The Co-operative Wholesale Societies were major customers and bought large numbers of NCB electric chassis and built their own bodies on many of them. The subtle differences of these are evident in this 1947 built 14cwt mobile shop operated by the Cleadon branch of the Boldon Co-op, in county Durham. Note the early South Shields telephone number. *(Turner's [Photography] Ltd)*

the direction of HW Heyman, who arrived at NCB in 1946. Heymann had been apprenticed to AEG in Berlin, later moving to Electricars in Birmingham and then Metropolitan Vickers in Sheffield where he was involved in design work for the Air Ministry and the Admiralty for the war effort. He joined Brush when that company purchased Metro-Vick's interest in electric vehicles in 1945. This enabled Hatton to devote more time to bus body development and production.

The chassis of the new vehicle was to consist of deep channel sections of mild steel, welded together to form a strong rigid support for the batteries, mounted on the sides between the wheels, and the motor was located centrally to drive the rear axle. The frame was dropped ahead of the front axle to give a low entrance to the cab for the driver. The British Thompson Houston Co (BTH) manufactured the motor and electrical control equipment. The motor was based on one designed during the war for use in 'midget' submarines. Chloride supplied the 'Exide' lead acid batteries, mounted in easily removable crates, to supply the power. The cab was coachbuilt to a standard simple and attractive design, with steering wheel, controller (accelerator), on/off/reverse switch and brake, as the only controls needed. Various body configurations were available according to the requirements of the customer, the most popular being the open sided milk float. When painting into customer's livery was required, this was carried out at Claremont Road.

The largest customer was the Co-operative Wholesale Society, who individually inspected every vehicle before delivery. The Co-op also bought many in chassis form, and built and painted the bodies in their own workshops. Accordingly they became a familiar sight in many parts of the British Isles, delivering Co-op milk and groceries.

Another significant customer who helped to establish the NCB battery-electric vehicle business was Thomas & Evans of Porth, in the Rhondda valley. This firm had developed along the same lines as Ringtons Tea, by building up a loyal clientele in Wales, with door to door deliveries of 'Corona' soft drinks.

Below: One of the earliest production electric vans was built with left-hand drive for demonstration on the continent. A 10/15cwt model, it retained the complicated roof curvature and bowed front dash of the prototype, but the square cornered windows were adopted for all future versions. It is seen here in October 1948 in Liege, Belgium, in service with a local laundry. Note the lady driver shown in this publicity picture, to emphasise the ease of control in the days when this was regarded as a man's job. *(Turner's [Photography] Ltd)*

It would have been unthinkable for the parent Ringtons company to fail to operate one of the new BEVs. This three-quarter ton short-wheelbase version shows the style of bodywork finally adopted for production. The livery was a very attractive green and black with gold sign writing. It was photographed outside the NCB works in the Team Valley Trading Estate, Gateshead, in 1947.
(Turner's [Photography] Ltd)

The one-ton model was recognised by the slightly larger body 'stepped out' from the cab. In 1947 this one was carrying a special load consisting of a ton of heavy coiled wire for acceleration and brake tests in Clara Street, Newcastle, a typical nineteenth century street with terraced houses, sloping steeply down to the river Tyne, with Dunston Power Station, Gateshead, in the background. The customer, The North of Scotland Milk Marketing Board, took delivery of a large fleet of similar vehicles. Note the NCB trade-plate (044 BB) carried during these tests.
(Turner's [Photography] Ltd)

Electric vehicles were first used for 'Corona' in 1939, and from 1946 a large fleet of over 200 NCB vehicles was built up. In 1947 Crown Motors (Thomas & Evans) Ltd was appointed distributor and agent for NCB electric vehicles in Wales. Corona drinks became nationally known before the end of the decade.

A number of tests were conducted by NCB during this period, using battery-electrics in actual service over rounds normally operated by petrol engined milk floats. In every case, the electric vehicle was quicker, in one case by about two hours. The roundsmen liked them too, finding their simple controls, ease of entry and acceleration gave them a much more relaxed driving experience. Tests were also conducted against the vehicles made by other manufacturers, and the company was satisfied that the NCB versions were in most cases superior to those of the competition.

During 1947, BTH announced that 500 sets of battery-electric equipment were on order. At about the same time, NCB announced that it was to enter into a joint development with Walkers of Wigan, a specialist builder of municipal refuse collectors and mobile cranes. The new joint agreement was for Walkers to construct a suitable five-ton chassis, which NCB would then complete with the electrical equipment and batteries.

A one-and-a-half ton NCB van, intended for the delivery of dairy products, laundry, parcels or for use as a travelling shop, was shown at Earls Court in 1948, with a completely new and stylish cab. Sliding

The sturdy battery-electric chassis were supplied to the bodybuilder in this form. Note the arrangement of the batteries and position of the traction motor in this 14cwt version, allowing easy access for routine maintenance. All the driving equipment was carried on the front dash, thus simplifying the work needed to build the bodywork.
(Turner's [Photography] Ltd)

The wider body of the **NCB** battery-electric one-ton version is typified by this Gateshead Co-op milk float. *(Turner's [Photography] Ltd)*

The prototype two-ton van is seen here after returning to the factory after exhibition at Earls Court in September 1948, hence the 'NCB 301' registration plate fitted for the show. Though in Co-op livery, it was owned by **NCB** who used it as a demonstrator. Most of these larger models were put to use as travelling shops, a popular concept at that time. *(Turner's [Photography] Ltd)*

doors were fitted to both sides, allowing the driver to leave them open on busy stretches of the delivery round. Another innovation was a tip-up driving seat that allowed the vehicle to be driven while standing up. Like the bus bodies, the cab was jig built for ease of construction and repair. It utilised aluminium framework, with aluminium panels lined with plywood. There was provision for a third sliding door to be situated behind the driver when required, enabling him to access the van interior without leaving the vehicle.

Lockheed hydraulic brakes were fitted, and additionally a new safety feature designed by NCB engineers was added. This was the 'Electropark', a solenoid operated braking device controlled by a switch or push-button. It was not then unknown for small boys (and some not so small!) to release the hand brake while the driver was making a delivery; the vehicle would then run away. The 'Electropark' switch held the brakes on and isolated the controller, while the push-button allowed the driver to hold the vehicle on a gradient at traffic lights, and prevented 'roll-back'.

The prototype chassis was built at Team Valley, then taken to Claremont Road where the body was designed and built. After thorough and comprehensive testing, the new model was found to be capable of carrying a load of two tons, and subsequently many were built with this capacity. Apart from painting, that was the last involvement with battery-electric vehicles at that factory.

The new Walker-NCB five-ton refuse collector vehicle, anticipated since the announcement of the previous year, was also shown at Earls Court. Provided with a telescopic hydraulic ram to compress the refuse, two 12¼hp electric motors could power the vehicle at up to fifteen miles per hour, and a range of forty miles was claimed. The usual NCB rear axle ratio was 12 to 1, but to cope with the additional weight, an additional reduction gearbox was added, giving a transmission ratio of 20 to 1. At least three similar vehicles were built before Walker's ceased production in 1949, after which no more were produced.

The London Electricity Board was an early customer, finding the 14 cwt. NCB vans not only appropriate to their business, but handy and economical little runabouts in the busy London traffic. They operated in this eye-catching 'Central London Electricity' livery, these two were photographed at Team Valley before delivery in 1947. *(Turner's [Photography] Ltd)*

A much more severe design was adopted for the Walker/NCB refuse collector. In this it closely resembled other Walker products, and similar vehicles by other manufacturers. The prototype, completed in September 1948, clearly demonstrates the crew cab and the roller shutter door for the tool locker. *(Turner's [Photography] Ltd)*

Corona would deliver four large bottles of soft drinks every week to every customer on the round of this one ton delivery van, pictured in 1949. This is just one of the large fleet of identical vehicles for this south Wales operator, for whom delivery had commenced in 1946, and continued into the 1950s. *(Turner's [Photography] Ltd)*

Dobbin, BC! This view illustrates the old order and the new, as Dobbin casts a sceptical eye over the new NCB electric milk float which will bring about his retirement in British Columbia in 1948. Clean, quiet and efficient certainly, but some of the character will be lost at Jersey Farms, Vancouver, Canada. Built entirely at Gateshead, this left-hand drive vehicle illustrates the world wide market sales achieved by NCB battery-electrics in the 1940s. This success was maintained after the BEV production was separated into Smiths Electric Vehicles Ltd in 1949. *(K Challoner)*

8 – Rationalisation

A Standard Double-Decker

Returning to 1944, the NCB bus design team was taking a long hard look at what their post-war double-deck bus should look like. First of all, the sound design of the utility structure had proved itself. It was decided to adopt this unchanged, except that, of course, all the square corners and flat profiles would be removed. This structure was known in the trade as 'composite', because unlike early wood coachwork, it utilised a large amount of metal as well. The underframe was built from wood, which was then supported on both sides of each cross member with mild steel plates. The upright pillars had a longitudinal saw-cut part way through; into these saw cuts were forced steel flitch plates to add strength. All exterior panelling was of aluminium sheets, formed shaped and welded where necessary for domes and corners.

It had been intended that the post-war design would incorporate steel framing, not composite, and the various advertisements in the trade press in 1944 clearly showed that this was the case, with a drawing of the proposed steel pillar section and the provisional patent number as shown below This design was granted a full patent in 1947, under the names of Northern Coachbuilders Ltd and HW Hatton. In the event, a steel framed bus body was never built by NCB after the war. This may have been due to lack of time and design facilities, but it is more likely to have been because of the severe shortage of steel, which was 'rationed' by the Ministry of Supply. In addition, NCB did not have the heavy machinery to form and press the sections into shape.

Below: The 1947 patent pillar section referred to in the text. (Geoff Burrows collection)

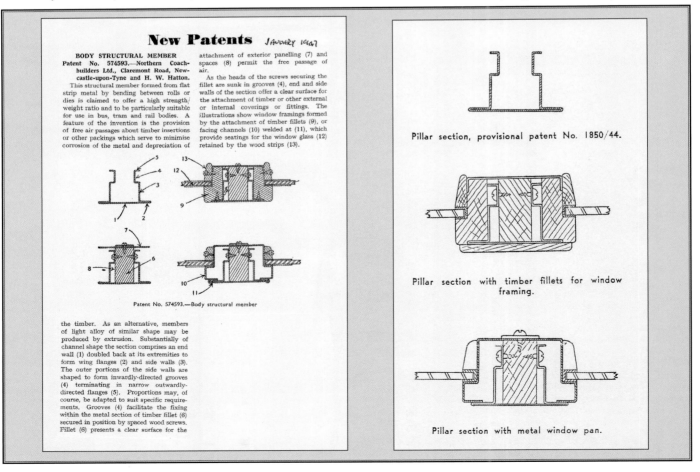

The profiles that had been drawn for the Bradford trolleybuses were studied and it was decided that the lower deck waist panel was too high, giving an out of proportion perspective. The front end also needed attention, to be smoothed out as in the London version, but with different detail. The Bradford style of rear end was considered rather upright, and the profile was given a gentle sweep. By this time, it was realised that the overall appearance was going to resemble the 1939 Weymann design very closely. A subtle difference was adopted, instead of the upper deck front window shape being created by overhanging rain shields, the window pans themselves were shaped, and so came the distinctive look that could immediately be recognised as – NCB. The end result closely resembled the shape of the double-deckers supplied to Merthyr Tydfil in 1939. The distinctive top deck emergency window with tapered sides was also re-adopted, though this time it was narrower, almost identical to that used on the London trolleybuses. The NCB version only differed by having square bottom corners. This became an instantly recognisable NCB 'trademark'.

Horace Hatton's most important input into the design was to lower the centre of gravity by using aluminium framing to reduce the weight of the roof. A pre-formed structure was produced, using aluminium panels riveted to aluminium cross members or 'hoop-sticks'. This was jig built and lifted onto the upper deck, once the body framing had been completed. The gangway was also lowered for an inch or so between the chassis members. This reduced the

NCB bodies were recognisable by the shape of the emergency exit, as seen here on Northampton's Daimler CVG6 of 1948, and now preserved. *(John A Senior)*

height in both highbridge and lowbridge bodies, but was not possible on those trolleybuses where the motor was situated under the centre of the gangway.

'Widney' patented glazing was adopted for all the main glazing, proprietary equipment was bought for the cab windows to suit the different shapes and sizes of radiators and engine compartments. For trolleybuses an attractive dropped waistline at the front was combined with shaped and dished panels to accommodate the double windscreen. There was sufficient space inside the upper deck front bulkhead to place most types of destination equipment without having to resort to projecting it forward of the front profile. A projecting destination box was sometimes necessary at the back of the bus, because the box containing the blinds and winding equipment could not be allowed to obstruct the staircase and handrails.

The low gangway floor on the lower deck allowed the headroom to be brought down to the minimum, but there was a problem at the extreme front end. On motorbuses, the clutch housing projected through the bulkhead; this caused no difficulty, but directly behind this the gearbox was at floor level and so higher than the dropped main gangway. There was then insufficient height from floor to ceiling to meet the regulations. The problem was solved by inserting a concave roof panel at the front, which raised the height in this area.

Internally, the vehicles were finished to the high standards that were required by operators. White ceiling and cove panels on both decks were secured by polished wood capping, also used around the windows. This was known as a 'double skin', something that not all coachbuilders supplied at that time. This reduced the amount of internal condensation, which was not only unsightly but also added unnecessarily to the problem of corrosion.

Below the waist, internal aluminium panels were covered with Rexine to the customer's choice of colour, though some operators preferred a stove enamelled finish. Unless the operator specified differently, the interior lamps were enclosed in neat translucent shades, and bell pushes were flush fitted into round 'finger plates' to protect the ceiling panels. Seats were of tubular construction, with stainless top rails and corner grab handles, upholstered in any style and combination of moquette, Rexine or leather that the customer chose. Handrails were to the customer's choice of stainless steel or coloured acetate. On trolleybus bodies, it was a legal requirement that the handrails on the platform, which the passenger could reach from the pavement, must always be plastic-covered to prevent possible electric shock on wet days, when very occasionally 'current leakage' could occur.

A problem that faced all bus bodybuilders was that of the varying lengths of the bonnet assembly. Because of the different lengths of engines and the way the chassis builders mounted them, the distance of the rear dash panel (behind the driver) from the front of the bus varied considerably. This was part of the chassis assembly, and it meant that the amount of space between the two lower saloon bulkheads was sometimes reduced so much that it was difficult to fit in the seats while maintaining the legal minimum spaces between them. Various methods were used to achieve this, such as by making the seat backs almost vertical, but sometimes even this did not work, and particularly so on tall seats fitted with grab rails. It was then necessary to make wooden wedges to go under the back feet of the seats, thus tipping them forward! There were also other, shall we say, 'temporary' methods employed on the days of the Certifying Officers visits, which were afterwards 'rectified'!

Window length was also affected by this problem, and this, of course, affected both decks. The method chosen by Northern Coachbuilders was to have the first four windows of standard length, the fifth was modified to suit the available space. This procedure had been adopted from the earliest utility designs and had proved invaluable in simplifying construction on the many varied chassis being rebodied.

In preparation for the anticipated amount of work that would come after the end of the war, the Claremont Road factory was gradually re-organised by the management for the manufacture of bus bodies, following the end of glider production in 1945. The facilities at Cramlington were very basic, and it was decided to end manufacture there. This gave the company some much-needed space for the storage and drying of timber, and to hold customers' chassis while they were waiting to be bodied. At Claremont Road the works was divided into specific areas, so that bare chassis would enter at one door, progress around the factory and emerge from another as a complete bus. (See diagram on page 26 for the factory layout.)

The first area was the Assembly Shop, where the chassis was prepared to receive the body by the removal of the batteries and other fittings that could interfere with the bodybuilding, and fitting the mounting brackets for the cross members. The body sections were built in this shop, using jigs for nearside and offside upper and lower deck side frames, top deck front and rear ends, the complete intermediate floor, top deck roof, front and rear bulkheads and lower deck rear end frames. The jigs were adjustable, to accommodate the various body lengths and the 30ft 0in trolleybus version.

The intermediate floor consisted of a composite framework, this was first covered with a diagonal layer of tongued and grooved ('t&g') creosoted softwood, then sealed with tarred paper, followed by a final layer of 't&g', laid diagonally to the original layer. The result was a strong, waterproof floor.

Construction proper now began. Body underframes and platforms were built directly onto the chassis, due to the number and complexity of variations. The bulkheads were fitted to the underframe, then sideframes, intermediate floor, rear end and platform. A further jig was used to assemble the already completed upper deck sides, ends and roof, thus completing the upper deck structure. This was then lifted clear of the jig and lowered onto the bottom deck and secured.

The bus was then moved into the Body Shop, where it was transformed from a bare frame into a recognisable shape. This was done by the addition of driver's cab, staircase (another jig built item), exterior panels, window pans, glazing, strapping, mouldings and beadings. Then finishing detail work commenced, this meant interior panels, floor covering, electrical wiring and lighting, handrails and all the other finishing touches. All the appropriate interior panels were stove enamelled before assembly into the vehicles, and all the wood cappings were painstakingly polished and varnished.

Lastly the seats were installed and the bus was moved into the Paint Shop ready for the exterior finishing. The process began by filling any panel imperfections with 'stopping', then six coats of paint were brushed on by hand, each being rubbed down with 'wet and dry' paper, used 'wet'. A signwriter then put on any lining and lettering that was required, and the various transfers such as fleet numbers and 'No Smoking' notices. The bus was then put into the Varnish Room for a final coat of varnish, after which it would emerge gleaming and ready for final inspection. Woe betide any unauthorised person who tried to enter the Varnish Room!

Finally, every bus was taken outside the factory for a thorough dousing with water from a hosepipe for half an hour, while an inspector searched for leaks inside. This was followed by a road test, during which Chief Inspector 'Wiggie' Stobbs searched for any undue body noises or movement. A visit to the weighbridge would be included in the excursion.

Chief Inspector Stobbs liked the new buses to be bounced along roads with tram tracks, as these were usually fairly rough due to wartime neglect. After these tests, any rectification work found to be necessary was completed. It was also common practice for the customer to visit the works during construction, to comment on or criticise the work and progress.

The new vehicle was then given an appointment with the Ministry of Transport Certifying Officer, who had to approve every bus before it left the factory. He assessed it against a table of legal requirements for all aspects, not only for things like length and width, but spacing between seats, position of fuel fillers, lights and the absence of dangerous sharp corners. If the bus was the first of its kind, for example on a type of chassis that had not previously carried an NCB body, then he would order a tilt test.

In this case the bus would be driven to the Newcastle Corporation Transport main works at Byker, where there was a tilt platform. After the bus had been mounted on it, the equivalent weight in sandbags of a full load of passengers would be placed on the upper deck, and the platform was tilted sideways to an angle of 28°, in the presence of Ministry of Transport officials. If the bus kept all its wheels on the platform then it had passed! As a safety precaution, padded guard chains were slung over the bus, but they were never needed for a bus built by NCB. In 1947 the company designed its own tilt test platform. The parts were manufactured at Claremont Road, and it was erected at Cramlington, where subsequent tilt tests were carried out. It should be mentioned here that the tilt tests in pre-war days had also been carried out at NCT's Byker works.

Usually, after all this the Certifying Officer would then issue the Certificate of Fitness for the bus, but one day he had different ideas. He had got it into his

As explained in the text, the first Daimler CVG6 chassis built went for export; and the first for a British operator went to Northampton Corporation in 1947, with NCB bodies. The delivery of the 20 vehicles began in June 1947, and one of them was often seen in NCB publicity pictures, shown on the tilt test platform at the Daimler works in Coventry for the purpose. Seen in the picture, left to right, are the two certifying officers, Mr J Cooper, Northampton's Manager, Horace W Hatton, and Mr D Boxall from the Daimler company. Number 154 from this batch survives in preservation. *(Transport Vehicles [Daimler] Ltd)*

head that it was possible for the rear platform to 'ground' in certain conditions. He thought that it might just touch the road surface when cornering at speed. Perhaps he had experienced a bad journey that day! He asked for as many apprentices as could be spared to stand on the platform and 'bounce'. You can imagine the expressions on the faces of the managers as this took place. Despite the apprentices sweating through exertion, and the managers perspiring for other reasons, it proved impossible to make any part of the platform touch the factory floor. The exercise seems to have had little point, because the legal height requirement for the platform in the unladen condition was a minimum of 10in, and a maximum of 17in, and this was easily checked with a tape measure.

At this point, the authors have found that they are quite unable to convey to the reader the wonderful smell of a new bus of that era. It was composed of a combination of new wood, paint and leather, and to board one for the first time was an unforgettable and unique experience. Even in a wartime utility the smell of varnish on the wooden seats on a vehicle making its first day's journey was pleasantly unforgettable. The buses of today don't have it, and even fully restored old buses seem to lack the magic recipe that created the original aroma.

To support all this activity, the works included a Woodmill, Panel Shop, Blacksmiths Shop, Electricians Shop, Tinsmiths Shop, Stores, Machine Shop, Trim Shop (upholstery room) Tool Store and Drawing Office. All the parts and components were identified with part numbers during manufacture. Not only did this assist the stores management, but also facilitated the speedy supply of spares for customers. There were, of course, all the usual offices for Management, Sales and Accounts, and next door to the factory was a Works Canteen, very necessary in the days of rationing and food shortages.

A small area of the workshop had been retained for what was previously an important part of the firm's business in its early days, the construction and repair of commercial vehicles. Very commendably, NCB kept its faith with the local firms who had supported them in the past. As early as 1945, a platform body was built on a Guy Vixant chassis, which was one of the first commercial vehicle chassis to go on sale at the end of the war. There was really insufficient space at Claremont Road, and so substantial premises of 700 square feet at Benfield Road were obtained, to which this work was transferred. A body shop and paint spray booth was set up, and a large yard at the back was useful for vehicle storage.

Not only were such items as platform lorries and cabs built, but maintenance and repair work was also carried out. One contract was with the Milk Marketing Board, for cleaning out and refurbishing their large fleet of road tankers. This was not a pleasant task, as the motion of the vehicles on the road turned them into gigantic milk churns after a while. Lorry cabs for Leyland trucks were built which closely resembled the original designs of the chassis builders. Among the customers were Sinclair, a Newcastle tobacco wholesaler, who required a number of vans, and four Leyland Comet trucks for Armstrong of Team Valley, for their floor tile business. Newcastle Breweries, who are world famous, bought some platform trucks for beer transport. Taylor's Foundry of South Shields was another customer for a Leyland platform truck. This was used for the carriage of very heavy loads of pig iron, and finished cast iron ships' propellers.

9 – Resumption

Early Post-War Sales

The year 1946 saw a further increase in activity and interest at Northern Coachbuilders. A change to the management team saw Horace Beck from Titanine paint specialists join as Sales Manager. The final utility buses had been completed at Cramlington, and the last bodies to be produced there were the 20 trolleybuses for London. With the end of the glider production, the scene was set for the return of bus manufacture to Claremont Road. It began with the Bradford trolleybuses to their interim design. These were all on chassis that had been stripped of their old bodies, either by intent or by Herr Hitler.

The new Bradford trolleybus bodies, of composite construction with oak framing and ash pillars, were given direct rubber mounted glazing of the same type as the utility bodies. The push-in window ventilators at the front of the top deck gave them a very 'severe' appearance. As already recounted, the characteristic emergency window glass shape distinguished the rear end.

The six Bradford vehicles were completed at Claremont Road between June and October 1946, and painted in that city's attractive light-blue and cream livery, with grey roofs. The interiors, though austere compared with their previous bodies, were nicely finished, fitted with their original seats following re-upholstery in moquette and leather, and with light varnished wood forming the window surrounds.

The contemporary trade press stated that the Bradford trolleybus chassis had been refurbished after the removal of their old bodies, ready for their new ones. When they arrived in Newcastle, there were many areas of rust and

Horace Beck

The six Bradford trolleybus bodies completed at Claremont Road between June and October 1946 represented a welcome return to something approaching normality from the factory with their attractive livery, lined out in gold, and more normal body styling after the numerous utility vehicles which had been produced. *(James Riddell)*

damage, and large accumulations of mud. Some chassis still had pieces of their old underframes and mounting brackets attached. The NCB engineers spent hours on these chassis bringing them into a fit mechanical state to receive their new bodies. Once this work was complete, a protective coat of aluminium paint was applied. Presumably Bradford paid due attention to the motors and electrical equipment on the return of the completed trolleybuses to their home city, because they remained in service for many years after rebuilding. The Bradford trolleybus bodies were still in production when the first of the new post-war standard bodies were completed.

In January 1945, the Northern General Transport Company had ordered six 'wartime standard double-deck bodies' from NCB, to cost £6,132. The order was modified in May for one of the bodies to go to the Tyneside fleet. Five of the chassis were the 'short' version of the AEC Regent, built in 1932 (including the Tyneside unit), and the sixth chassis was the only Northern 'SOS' double-decker, type REDD. They were sent to Claremont Road where 985 (FT 2523) received the prototype body of the new post-war design in the spring of 1946. The remainder of the order, and all future double-deck production was to this design; no more utility bodies were laid down. The Bradford trolleybus bodies were still in production when these new post-war bodies were built.

The next customer to receive a quantity of the new post-war standard bodies was Bolton Corporation, whose first order with NCB had been placed in October 1944. This initial order was made under the Ministry of Supply allocation system, and was for five utility bodies, increased to six in January 1945. They were to be mounted on reconditioned Leyland TD4c chassis. A second order was placed by Bolton in March 1945 for another twelve new bodies, to be mounted on a mixture of nine TD3, TD3c and TD4c double-deck chassis, and three Leyland Tiger TS7c single-deck chassis converted to double-deck dimensions. The order also called for five existing bodies to be rebuilt by NCB. All the new bodies for the first order and one for the second were completed in July 1945, to full utility pattern. (See illustration on page 168.)

Then Bolton ordered a further four new bodies in October 1945, again for TD3, TD3c and TD4c chassis. Delays to the single-deck conversions were caused by Ministry paperwork. Other problems, including the condition of some of the chassis and engines, meant that no more new bodies reached Bolton until December 1945; when they did they were of the relaxed version with more opening windows and rounded rear domes. Six were delivered between then and March 1946.

The earliest municipal operator of the post-war standard NCB bodywork was Bolton. They were all fitted to pre-war Leyland chassis. Later several of these bodies were transferred to other chassis, when the original chassis were scrapped. Seen here is 212 (AWH 950), a Leyland TD5 of 1940, carrying the body which had been fitted to the 1933 Leyland TD3c chassis of 76 (WH 4905). It was finally withdrawn in 1957. (Roy Marshall)

Facing page: When NGT received the prototype body of the new post-war design in the spring of 1946, it was fitted to 985 (FT 2523). The specification of the 1932 AEC Regent chassis was very little different from the new AEC chassis being produced immediately after the end of the war. Consequently, NGT knew that there was still much useful life left in the examples in its fleet, and the re-bodying exercise produced virtually new vehicles at a time of severe shortage. (James Riddell)

Right: This photograph is of poor quality, but the authors feel that it is important enough to show it. NGT 593 (HA 8002) was the only double-deck SOS in the NGT fleet, bought from Midland Red in 1933 with a Short Bros body. As noted in the text, it was one of the first buses to receive a post-war standard NCB body, in 1945. The chassis was scrapped in 1952, and the NCB body was transferred to a former City of Oxford AEC Regent (EWL 749), now NGT 1395. (Geoff Burrows collection)

This 4mm scale drawing has been specially prepared for this book by Gerry Bixley for use by modellers. It shows the standard NCB highbridge body, fitted to new post-war AEC Regent chassis for Northern General in 1946. With a few adjustments this drawing can be adapted for any of the post-war standard NCB body customers. (Geoff Burrows collection)

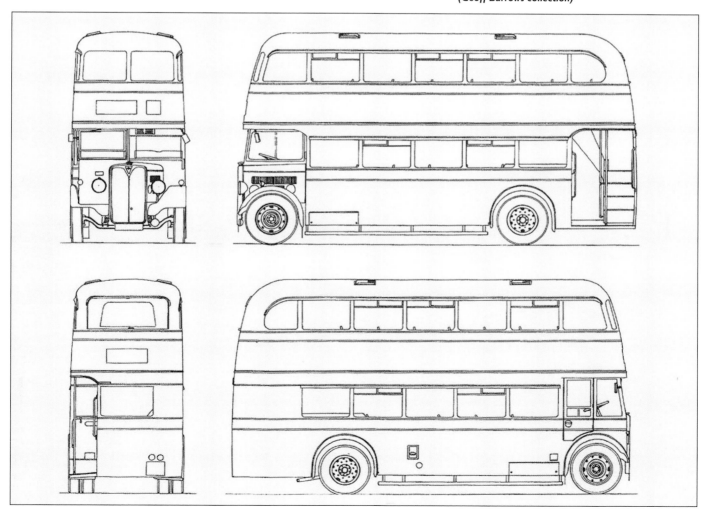

Meanwhile, in February 1946, Bolton received a letter from NCB informing the Corporation that the remaining nine bodies of the two outstanding orders would be built to the new post-war design and, consequently, there would be a delay in making the deliveries. It is recorded that the Bolton management was less than pleased by this. There was also a price increase, which pleased them even less. The first NCB post-war standard body for Bolton was delivered in July 1946. The remaining eight, including the converted single-deck chassis, were eventually sent to Bolton and the orders were completed by October 1946.

To try to overcome these vicissitudes the NCB salesman responsible for the Bolton contracts worked hard to maintain a friendly relationship between the Bolton management and NCB. He asked the Chairman of the Bolton Transport Committee on several occasions to enjoy a weekend 'on the town' in Newcastle. This invitation was never accepted, but the gentleman in question did visit a local hostelry in the company of representatives of a coachbuilder much nearer to his home.

The very first new standard bodies to be built on new chassis were appropriately for Northern General, towards the end of the year. There were ten AEC Regents, (ACN 167-176), and the only post war chassis of that type for the parent Northern General company. They were followed immediately by the first of many post-war Guy Arabs for Northern, and they became the company's standard double-deck buses until 1949.

Early 1947 saw twelve Guy Arabs delivered to the Lancashire municipality Blackburn Corporation in their smart dark green dignified livery with cream waist bands on both decks and cream window frames on the lower deck, complete with ornate black and gold lining out. Unfortunately, ACB 901-912 were badly afflicted by 'green timber', and most of them had to be returned for some fairly severe rectification work. In their rebuilt form, they worked out full lives, and a number survived to be sold for further service elsewhere.

Another large contract started that year was for 24 bodies on Daimler CWD6 and CVD6 chassis for Aberdeen, (BRS 556/558-581). Delivered in 1946 and 1947, these buses showed the new design to its best advantage. Internally, the ceilings were given coloured patterned panels known as 'Alhambrinal'. Externally, their Brunswick green and ivory paint was devoid of all except black lining, but very smart for all that. With supreme confidence the 'fleet name' was painted in large black letters on the lower deck waistband, 'CORPORATION TRANSPORT', without

A snowy day in December 1946 shows another Daimler, this time model CVD6, for the second major Scottish customer, Dundee. There were twenty, and No. 35 (YJ 9039) leaves the onlooker in no doubt about who is proud to own the city's buses. The green and white livery was embellished with ornate gold, orange and black lining out, and inside they also had 'Alhambrinal' ceiling panels (see the advertisement above) and hand-tooled leather seat covering. Most of this batch was still in use twenty years later after being rebuilt in the operator's workshops.
(Turner's [Photography] Ltd)

A large contract was started in 1946 for 24 bodies on Daimler chassis for Aberdeen. The ceilings were again given coloured patterned panels known by the trademark 'Alhambrinal', and leather covered seats were fitted. The interior lighting was fitted with 'moonstone' translucent shades, the standard **NCB** fitting. *(James Riddell)*

Early 1947 saw twelve **Guy Arabs** delivered to Blackburn Corporation. Those with long memories will recall that 1947 saw the worst winter in decades and Blackburn's sombre green livery did not take kindly to those conditions when it was photographed, the accumulated snow and ice in the opposite gutter reflecting in the new paintwork. They were probably the last 'long' Arabs to be built. The long mudguards of the Arab came in useful when there was time for a cigarette between duties, as seen in the lower view, but Leyland seem to be outgunning Guy to some tune here.
(Turner's [Photography] Ltd), Michael Dryhurst)

Top: Tom Severn bought this Leyland PD1 for his service from the Yorkshire village of Stainforth. Severn was one of a number of small independents operating to Doncaster; Felix purchased a similar body on an AEC Regent and Premier did likewise utilising a Guy Arab.
(Turner's [Photography] Ltd)

Below: Three of these Daimler CVD6s highbridge buses were supplied to Truman of South Normanton, Derbyshire.
(Turner's [Photography] Ltd)

the name of the city. Twenty very similar buses were built for another Scottish city during 1947, on Daimler CVD6 chassis. On the upper deck waist panels where advertisements were usually shown, there was a large black and gold underlined fleetname 'DUNDEE'. These buses (YJ 9039-9058) were also green and cream, but a much lighter shade than that used by Aberdeen, attractively finished with very complicated coloured lining out and again the words 'Corporation Transport' on the waist.

At this point in history, the Ministry of War Transport was relinquishing its control on the allocation of vehicles, but numbers of buses were still in the system for customers who had been allocated NCB bodies. However, this was not the case for twelve trolleybus bodies for Maidstone Corporation. Horace Hatton, the chief engineer at NCB, had previously worked in a similar capacity for many years at Brush Coachworks Ltd, Loughborough. Mr CS Johnstone, the General Manager at Maidstone, had also worked at Brush in the drawing office during the same period. Mr Johnstone was appointed General Manager at Maidstone on 1st January 1946. Later in that same month the tender of Northern Coachbuilders to build the bodies for twelve Sunbeam W chassis already allocated to Maidstone was accepted by that corporation, which when built became HKR 1-12.

When ordering these vehicles, it had not been appreciated by the operator that the amount of ventilation provided on modern buses was far less than the ancient trolleybuses that they were replacing. Consequently, on their first summer in service, temperatures inside rose to resemble that in a greenhouse. Maidstone Corporation then asked NCB to fit and pay for additional ventilation. NCB offered to supply hinged ventilators for the upper deck front windows, and quite rightly pointed out that these and any additional work would have to be at Maidstone's expense. Maidstone declined the offer, and instead modified the vehicles themselves by cutting long slots in the front domes and bending the metalwork out to form crude louvres.

Orders for trolleybus bodies in 1946 were very satisfactory. Following the initial six for Bradford, another eleven were ordered to replace old bodies, this time to the new standard design, and once again on AEC chassis. The two types were referred to as 'Mark I' and 'Mark II' in Bradford. Delivery of these was a protracted affair, as Bradford could not spare many trolleybuses to be out of service at the same time. This was followed by an order for another ten, and it was 1949 before they were all completed.

The Maidstone vehicles were smart looking in their light brown and cream livery as can be seen from the two official views on the facing page. Number 62 is shown before delivery with the works lorry in attendance, complete with apparently somewhat disinterested driver by the traction pole! This vehicle also featured in the series of advertisements illustrating users of NCB bodywork in the trade press as seen above. (JH Herdman collection)

Above: Following the initial six, Bradford ordered another eleven replacement trolleybus bodies, this time to the new standard design, and once again on AEC chassis. This photograph shows 630 (AAK 432), the first to be completed. It re-entered service in Bradford on 1st September 1947. *(Turner's [Photography] Ltd)*

Below: Bradford celebrated the jubilee of the trolleybus system in 1961, and painted two vehicles in earlier liveries. NCB-bodied 603 (KY 8206), a 1934 AEC with 1947 NCB body was given a replica of the original 1911 Prussian blue and broken white livery, complete with ornate gilt lining and classic fleet numbers. *(Alan Cross)*

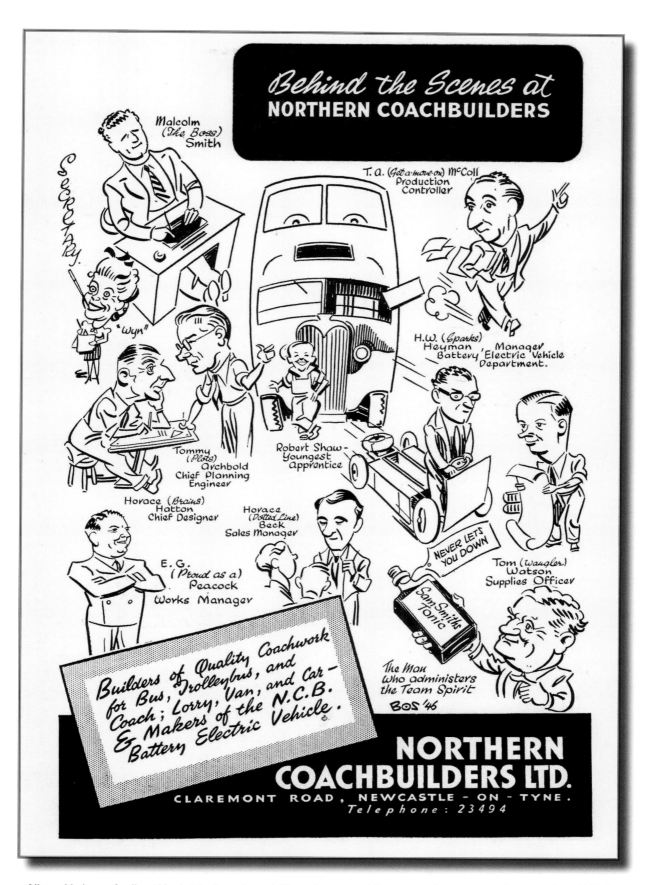

All one big happy family – this sketch, drawn by a staff member, accurately portrays the most prominent people at **NCB** in 1946. It appeared in the trade press during 1946. Horace Beck has recently joined **NCB** from Titanine Paints. This was the team responsible for the **NCB** rise in popularity. Robert Shaw can be seen in person on the left in the picture on page 107. *(JH Herdman)*

Northern Coachbuilders' Latest Models

SUNBEAM F.4. CHASSIS FOR SOUTH SHIELDS

THE trolleybus illustrated on this page is one of a number of Sunbeam F.4 two-axle vehicles, with Northern Coachbuilders' bodywork, recently supplied to South Shields Corporation. The body lines, particularly those of the top cover, have been much admired. Northern Coachbuilders, Ltd., will build the bodies for a further fleet of similar trolleybuses for South Shields, chassis for which have just been completed by Sunbeam Commercial Vehicles, Ltd. A further repeat order is also in hand.

team putting their best into the job. The forthright personalities of Mr. Malcolm Smith, managing director, Mr. E. G. Peacock, works manager and other members of the planning and production staffs, are reflected in the product—a good, solid body without frills, but with remarkably pleasing lines.

A section of the factory is devoted to development work. Northern Coachbuilders take the view that the only conclusive test of bodywork is in service, and experimental bulkheads, pillar sec-

★

One of the new South Shields trolleybuses, with Sunbeam chassis and Northern Coachbuilders' bodywork

★

Bodies for the 25 two-axle trolleybuses recently ordered from Sunbeam by Newcastle-upon-Tyne Corporation will be produced by Northern Coachbuilders, who are also constructing bodies for the 30 three-axle Sunbeam trolleybuses ordered by Newcastle in October, 1946. Three orders for Sunbeam trolleybuses have been placed by Newcastle Corporation since the end of the war, and the total number of chassis involved is 91.

Northern Coachbuilders have earned a reputation for a fundamentally sound composite body, and the impression gained from a visit to their Claremont Road works at Newcastle is of a happy

tions, etc., are incorporated in customers' vehicles on a guaranteed maintenance basis.

The battery vehicle department occupies premises on the Team Valley Estate, Gateshead, where the coachbuilding side has also planned a new factory. Battery vehicle production is under the control of Mr. H. W. Heyman, who has had exceptional experience with this form of transport. N.C.B. battery electrics have been adopted as standard by the Co-operative Wholesale Society, and important developments concerning Eire, New Zealand and the Argentine are expected.

Shown on the NCB tilt platform at Cramlington (designed by one of the authors) is one of the South Shields batch of ten 1947/8 Karrier W4s.
(J Herdman collection)

The moquette trimmed seats in the lower deck and leather upstairs are featured in the first NCB trolleybuses for South Shields. The internal wood cappings were merely varnished; french polishing had not yet been resumed. Projecting lamps with white reflectors are the operator's requirement. *(J Herdman collection)*

The third of the South Shields trio, 248, is seen here about to turn at the Marsden Inn roundabout for service 12 to the Market via Stadium. Note the later addition of the route number indicator by the operator. *(Senior Transport Archive)*

Below: A further ten Karrier W4 trolleybuses were built for South Shields in 1947. They were outwardly similar to the original batch apart from the indicator and route number box arrangement. St Hilda's church is the location of 255 in later days. *(Michael Dryhurst)*

In 1945 South Shields was allocated a batch of five Karrier 'W' chassis, but they were not built until late 1946. Three received standard NCB bodies in January 1947. Charles Roe of Leeds built the other two bodies to their semi-utility style. Consequently, the three NCB bodies looked really impressive with their curvaceous lines, and contrasted with the rather severe shape of the Roe bodies. The introduction of 246-8 (CU 4716-18) seen opposite, was to lead to more orders for NCB trolleybus bodies for South Shields, but regrettably none for their motor bus fleet.

Newcastle Corporation ordered 30 bodies in 1946 at £2,095 each for Sunbeam S7 three axle chassis, but it was not until 1948 that the chassis were received. They were given a 70-seat lengthened version of the standard body, incorporating a number of features that were special to the customer. One of these was the upper deck rear emergency window; the normal arrangement on a trolleybus was for the window to be hinged along the lower edge, and held in the open position by chains so as to lie horizontally. Then a specially designed platform would be taken out of its stowage behind the rear seat and clipped into position on the open window to enable staff to climb out onto the roof to attend to the trolley head equipment.

The Newcastle rolling stock engineer at that time was Mr R Edgley Cox, who later expanded the trolleybus system at Walsall when he became general manager there. Included in Cox's specification for the Newcastle bodies was a modified emergency window that had a fixed panel in the centre that would carry the weight of a man, with narrow vertical windows at each side. This arrangement was to be found on trolleybuses in Cardiff and St Helens, and obviated the need for the normal removable platform. Ten sets of components for the Newcastle trolleybuses had been made, and the first three were at an advanced stage of production when an inspection of work in progress was made by Mr FS Taylor, general manager at Newcastle, with some of his staff. Mr Taylor took an instant dislike to the emergency door arrangement, and

A happy occasion as the workforce poses with the first Newcastle Sunbeam trolleybus. Manager Frank Taylor said that he was well satisfied with the finished vehicles. *(Newcastle Journal)*

A Leyland Tiger PS1 and five Sunbeam S7 three-axle trolleybuses are seen in this view of the finishing and paint shop. At this stage the coachbuilders are inside the buses adding lining panels and seats. All exterior items such as lamps, handles and ventilators have been fitted and then removed so that the painters can apply the seven coats of paint that were given to the exterior of every bus, with each one rubbed down with 'wet and dry' paper. Even the wheels were removed before painting in the operators chosen colour.
(Bob Kell collection)

Newcastle three-axle trolleybuses shown under construction in the bodyshop in 1948. A completed staircase can be seen awaiting installation. (Newcastle Journal)

In this interior view note the '3+2' division of the longitudinal seats, and the single seat to allow access to the motor through the floor trap. *(Turner's [Photography] Ltd)*

ordered that the normal NCB window should replace it. It is not recorded what the reaction was or who paid for the re-work.

One of these trolleybuses, Newcastle No. 512, was displayed at the 1948 Commercial Motor Show at Earls Court in London, and was also frequently seen in NCB advertisements. Somewhat irreverently, the Newcastle trolleybus crews called them 'coffins', because they were long and narrow. The company was justifiably proud of these trolleybus bodies (LTN 499-528), and it is unfortunate that no further orders for the type were received, either from Newcastle or elsewhere. Certainly, they would have been suitable for Huddersfield, where 8ft 0in wide trolleybuses were never operated, and three-axle vehicles were standard.

It has often been erroneously stated that the upper deck pillars on trolleybus bodies had to be of stronger design than those for motorbuses. This theory, which may have been true on early vehicles, seems to be based on the fact that the front side pillars were often wider, giving the impression of a heavy structure. This was actually a pillar and a 'spacer' to accommodate the power wiring on its route from the trolley base on the roof, to the chassis. Some bodybuilders used the front centre pillar for this purpose, others used the front corners, but the majority, including NCB, chose the nearside upper deck pillar position, above the front bulkhead. The offside windows were then made to match, to equalise the window sizes. Then the heavy wiring was threaded through the bodywork to reach the electrical equipment and motor.

The 30ft 0in long Newcastle Sunbeam S7s had extra long platforms. The upstairs rear side windows ('D' lights) were of the NCB standard length, and the space was filled by a covering panel, which again appeared to be an extra heavy support. The trolley booms, which collected the electricity from the overhead wires were carried on steel gantries purchased from an outside specialist supplier, who designed them so that the fixings were situated on the roof above the pillars of the second window bay.

14th INTERNATIONAL

COMMERCIAL MOTOR TRANSPORT EXHIBITION

OCT 1-9

EARLS COURT

Seen under the wires on test and posed for the photographer Newcastle 499 (LTN 499) shone in the yellow livery. The long platform is evident in the lower view. *(Turner's [Photography] Ltd)*

Above: Prominent in this 1947 view of the main body shop at Claremont Road is a batch of Guy Arabs under construction for Yorkshire Woollen District Transport. In the centre foreground, the arch-shaped machines were used to 'wheel' the curved body panel shapes. A top deck roof framework and a top deck front can be seen, and in the right hand corner a battery-electric vehicle body is under development. The crowded working conditions did not make life easy for the skilled coachbuilders. Illustrating NCB experience and design ability are, from the left in the lower picture an early electric van for the large Corona order, the brewer's dray on a 1929 Leyland lorry chassis for the Sunderland Brewery, James Deuchar Ltd, and a Rington's tea van. In the background are two post-war double-deck buses for AEC Regent chassis of Northern General Transport Ltd of Gateshead. *(Bob Kell collection both)*

A letter of intent was received by NCB in 1947 from the Gateshead Tramways Company for 72 trolleybus bodies of 7ft 6in width, to be mounted on Sunbeam F4 chassis, subject to parliamentary approval of a proposed Bill to replace their trams. The Bill was never presented, and the NCB order was never confirmed. The opportunity to see two operators sharing their overhead wires with NCB trolleybuses was thus lost.

It was double-deck motor buses that largely filled the factory from that time onwards. New orders came from all over England and Scotland. Guy Arabs continued their newfound popularity not only with more for NGT, but also 15 for Yorkshire Woollen District (HD 7811-7825), As mentioned earlier, Blackburn took 12 (ACB 901-912), and Green Bus Service of Rugeley, Staffordshire with

Northampton Corporation had previously chosen bodywork supplied by CH Roe of Leeds, but in early 1947 NCB was able to offer much quicker delivery, so 20 Daimler CVG6 chassis were bodied by them instead. The example shown is No. 151 (ANH 151). The radiator protruded ahead of the cab to accommodate the long Gardner 6LW engine, resulting in a very short window ahead of the rear bulkhead. The idiosyncratic but informative destination display was repeated at the back in a slightly protruding box as shown.
(JH Herdman collection)

This lowbridge Guy Arab was one of a pair supplied to Green Bus of Rugeley, Staffordshire in 1947. They bought a third identical bus in 1948. *(Turner's [Photography] Ltd)*

The Derbyshire colliery village of South Normanton was the home of independent operator E Naylor & Sons. This highbridge-bodied Guy Arab was a 'one-off' in the fleet. South Normanton should not, of course, be confused with Normanton in Yorkshire. *(Turner's [Photography] Ltd)*

three (NRE 542/3, PRE 882) as we have seen. The Northern General order consisted of 10 Guy Arabs with high radiators, Nos.1177-86 (GPT 977-86).

The very first Daimler CVG6s to go to a British operator had NCB bodies, and comprised the order for 20 that went to Northampton Corporation, with deliveries starting in June 1947. The Northampton models (ANH 150-169) were the first NCB bodies on which the difficulty of fitting 26 seats into the lower deck of a bus that had the very long Gardner 6LW engine was experienced. One of them was often seen in NCB publicity pictures, shown on the tilt test platform undergoing its official test. For many years, these were the only non-Roe-bodied vehicles in the Northampton fleet.

Closely following them were three Daimler CVG6s for Maidstone (JKO 638-640) painted in the same light brown and cream livery as their trolleybuses. The intermediate cant panel and lower deck waist panels were brown, and the remainder was cream, resulting in a surprisingly smart appearance. An enquiry for another six had to be turned away, because 8ft 0in wide buses were now required. Though NCB was developing these wider bodies, the designs were a long way from completion, and instead the Maidstone order went to Brush Coachworks of Loughborough.

Leyland Titan PD1 chassis was represented by seven for Hants & Sussex Motor Services, of which four were the first lowbridge buses to be built to the new design. The operator was so pleased with them that the Managing Director, Basil Williams, sent a letter of commendation to the company that was then

Seven Leyland Titan PD1 chassis for Hants & Sussex Motor Services received NCB bodies, of which four were the first lowbridge buses to be built to the new design. Hants & Sussex Managing Director Basil Williams is seen in the centre of the picture with the impressive 'Hants & Sussex' fleet name behind. To his right is Malcolm Smith, NCB Managing Director, and to his left is the tall figure of Horace Hatton, Chief Engineer. With his back to the front wheel is EG 'Ted' Peacock, Works Manager. Next to Hatton and facing the rear wheel is Frank Taylor, Newcastle General Manager, and at the extreme right of the picture, Horace Beck, Sales Manager is surveying the scene with Newcastle Transport Committee Chairman Councillor H Simms. *(Newcastle Journal)*

The 'large operator' appearance of the Hants & Sussex company is exaggerated by the huge fleetname and the deceptively high fleet number **LO57**. Nevertheless, these buses were beautifully turned out, including the gold lining, but such a finish came at a cost, of course. *(Turner's [Photography] Ltd)*

displayed on the works notice board. FCG 523-525 were highbridge, FCG 526-528 and FOR 837 were lowbridge models, one of which was displayed at Earls Court in 1948. All were painted in a smart red and maroon livery with cream relief. The huge 'Hants & Sussex' fleetnames painted on the sides in underlined gold and black, and the fleet numbers, LO52-58, gave the impression of a very large operator. In fact, Hants and Sussex was quite a small company, and had ordered the Leylands during the war to ensure early delivery after the end of hostilities. They had difficulty finding enough work for them, and hired some of them to other operators for long periods of time. One was Cardiff Corporation, who used two, FCG 524 and FOR 837 from November 1947 until May 1949.

In direct contrast to the war years when all the bodies were constructed on old chassis, apart from the Park Royal sub-contract, all the post-war bodies after the initial ones for the Northern group were built on new chassis. The exceptions were the second batch of trolleybuses for Bradford as previously mentioned, and one Guy chassis. The circumstances behind this last re-body were extremely sad. GP Holder (Charlton-on-Otmoor Services) was the operator of a bus service that ran in and around Bicester Garrison in Oxfordshire to Bicester town, principally for service personnel. In 1945 he was allocated a new Guy double-decker with a Park Royal utility body for the service.

When still only a few weeks old, it was approaching one of several ungated level crossings in the camp, used by army trains for the transport of stores. As was apparently usual, the bus was grossly overloaded, with passengers standing on both decks, the platform and staircase. At the last moment, the driver noticed that a train was coming and tried to brake, but with little effect due to the extra heavy load. He then tried to accelerate, but again, due to the load and the limited power of the Gardner five cylinder engine, he failed to clear the crossing before the train collided with the rear end of the bus. There were no deaths, but unfortunately there was a high number of casualties, with several people, including some young ATS girls, losing limbs. The body was a write-off, but the chassis was repaired and sent to NCB under the Ministry of Supply allocation scheme. Registered BUD 65, it was given a standard NCB body and returned to GP Holder with whom it operated for many years.

An order for 30 bodies for the City of Sheffield had been placed at the end of the war, to be distributed between the 'A' (Corporation) and 'B' (Joint Omnibus Committee) fleets, all on AEC Regent Mark III chassis. However, when the chassis became due, AEC was only to meet the delivery date for the first ten.

When AEC could only supply 10 out of 30 chassis ordered for Sheffield due in 1947, ten each of Daimler and Crossley chassis were ordered to complete the NCB body contract. Thus, the only Crossley chassis to receive NCB bodies were delivered to the steel city, nine for the Corporation fleet, including A588 (KWB 88) shown here, and one for the Joint Omnibus Committee fleet. The standard NCB body did not sit well with the low Crossley bonnet line, even though a deeper than normal windscreen was incorporated. The Sheffield buses were always smartly turned out in cream, navy blue and matt grey roof with fine lining out. On all the contemporary deliveries to Sheffield from other manufacturers, the route number blinds were situated above the twin destination blinds. On these NCB bodies, the number blinds were to the nearside of them as seen in this splendid official view. *(Turner's [Photography] Ltd)*

The ten AECs for Sheffield built in 1947 were well received in the city as well they might have been when looking at this photograph. Sheffield's attractive livery sits well on this handsome design. *(Turner's [Photography] Ltd)*

117

Sheffield promptly ordered replacements in the form of ten Daimler CVD6 and ten Crossley DD42/5 chassis. When the delivery from NCB was completed in 1948, it comprised AECs (KWB 48-50,81-87), Daimlers (KWB 866,881,910/1/4, KWE 29-32,38), and the only Crossleys to receive NCB bodies (KWB 11,88-96). (These were delivered to NCB only six weeks after being ordered.)

An interesting point about these bodies concerns the indicators; on all the contemporary deliveries to Sheffield, the route number blinds were situated above the twin destination blinds. On the NCB bodies, the number blinds were to the near side of them. Perhaps this was due to a failure of communications, or perhaps the customer wished to try an alternative arrangement.

The Daimler CVD6 chassis had a slightly lower frame height than the other makes, and all NCB bodies were built to a standard height from the top of the chassis frame. Sheffield Corporation found this combination of chassis and highbridge body low enough to be suitable for a route to Chesterfield that passed under a bridge at Dronfield, previously restricted to low height buses.

The Sheffield buses were painted in an attractive pale cream livery, with three navy blue bands at waist and cant panel levels, together with neat and subtle lining out. The lower deck seating was finished in green moquette, with the upper deck in red leather. The Sheffield Joint Omnibus Committee had been formed in 1930 to take over the routes and services previously worked by the railway company buses in the area, London, Midland and Scottish (LMS), whose livery was red, and LNER, which was green. The retention of these colours for the seats was a pleasant historical reminder.

Facing page: Photographs of NCB bodies featured in a 1946-8 series of advertisements. Then a later series, with the 'Passing Parade' example shown here, relied on sketches. (Geoff Burrows collection)

Three Daimler CVG6s for Maidstone Corporation were built in 1947. Number 75 (JKO 639) is seen showing the ventilation slot fitted by the corporation. The bus stop is outside the Rootes Group premises, built on the site of the former Tilling Stevens factory. (Michael Dryhurst)

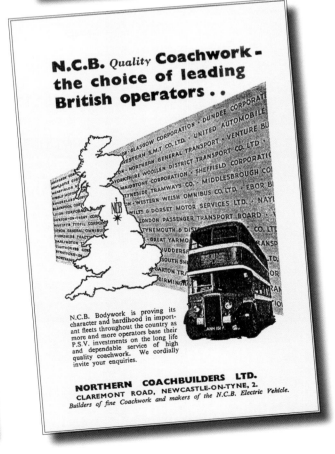

10 – Capitalisation

New Buses for London

The year 1946 could also have been marked in a really interesting way. London Transport found that the time taken to develop the new body for the RT buses had seriously jeopardised their bus replacement programme, and they desperately needed more new buses to replace the many old vehicles that were still soldiering on after the deprivations caused by the war. AEC and Leyland were able to meet all the chassis requirements, but the three bodybuilders who were contracted to build the RT bodies, Park Royal, Weymann and Metro-Cammell, were fully committed and could not make any improvements to their promised deliveries.

The following advertisement then appeared in the press, **'Applications are invited for the supply of up to one hundred 26ft 0in x 7ft 6in double-deck bus bodies for delivery in 1947 and before the end of 1948'.** London Transport also sent a similarly worded letter to 30 coachbuilders that they thought had the capability to meet their requirements.

In December 1946 those suppliers who had answered the advertisement and letters met LPTB officials in London. There were representatives from JC Beadle of Dartford, Cravens Ltd of Sheffield, Saunders Engineering and Shipbuilding whose factory was in Beaumaris on the Isle of Anglesey, the Acton-based Strachans (Successors) Ltd and Northern Coachbuilders. It is not known who represented NCB at the meeting.

Of these, only NCB had built any new buses recently for London Transport. Beadle was involved in the programme to recondition London's buses in the struggle to keep the wheels turning, Cravens had never built buses for London, and Strachans last bodies for London were the time-expired LTs and

What might have been ... Northern Coachbuilders decided against entering the lottery for a share of the newly extended RT contract. When an order was placed with Saunders, a standard Weymann example was sent to their Anglesey factory for examination by the design team. Saunders decided to build the bodies as nearly as practicable in appearance to the standard RT body but, using Saunders frame structure. As a result, the Saunders bodies were almost indistinguishable from the standard Park Royal/Weymann version. Below is shown the standard product, RT 1947 (LUC 33), built by Park Royal, photographed at Thornton Heath in 1961. This example, like all those built by Cravens and Saunders, is fitted with the distinctive route box in the front dome.
(Alan Cross)

STs built for the London General Omnibus Company in 1928-32. Saunders' highly successful programme of aircraft building was completed with the end of the war, and it was putting its workforce and skills to use in a new venture, the production of bus bodywork. In particular its expertise in working with aluminium, and patents held by the Company and by its director W Kemp.

Beadle offered to build 20 bodies, Cravens 120, Saunders 240 and Strachans 85, but NCB did not make an offer. In the event, LPTB placed orders for 120 bodies from Cravens, and 250 from Saunders, at a later date this was increased by a further 50. These orders were both in contradiction of the original stated requirement for 'up to 100 bodies'. Neither contractor met the delivery dates needed by London Transport. Difficulty with trying to meet these delivery dates was probably one reason that NCB did not become involved. The company may have been able to get around some of the problems by re-instating the Cramlington factory and using it in some form, but this would have taken time. Again, unlike Saunders and Cravens where there was already spare production capacity available, NCB would have had to find capital in order to buy equipment for the contract. This would have made it a highly speculative venture, with no certainty of continuity of work to use the extra facilities at the end of the London orders, especially perhaps since their relationship with LPTB was rather under a cloud over an advertising issue.

It is curious to realise that there was once a possibility that the standard NCB bodies could have been mounted on chassis with the famous 'RT' numbers on their bonnets. There is the precedent of the Cravens bodies to support this idea, because that company supplied its standard five bay bodies to London. One thing that the LPTB was insisting on was that the dimensions, detail and construction of the driver's cab and the platform and staircase should be exactly the same as the standard production RTs. This would not have presented a problem to NCB. Interestingly, after much thought and discussion, Saunders decided to produce a body identical in appearance to the standard RT, using their own method of construction.

Cravens offered a modified version of their own five-bay double-deck body. Incorporating the standard RT cab, platform, staircase and 'lighthouse' route number box with associated different destination display, the exterior was a reasonably close copy of the standard RT, enhanced by the same type of glazing. Internally they had a much more 'home-made' appearance. Presumably, NCB could have achieved much the same result with the same approach. Cravens factory is the setting for green RT 1402 (JXC 165). *(Courtesy Paul Fox)*

11 – Continuation

Business as Usual

In 1947 Bradford took delivery of 20 new motorbuses in their splendid blue and cream livery (EKU 524-543). The NCB bodies were mounted on AEC Regent III model 0961 chassis to full Bradford specification. Like many other early post-war deliveries, the Bradford chassis had been ordered in 1939, but the war had prevented earlier delivery. They were, in fact, amongst the first post-war Bradford buses, though delivery was not completed until 1948.

In April 1947, Huddersfield Joint Omnibus Committee also chose AEC chassis for six similar buses (ECX 420-425). Their lowbridge bodies were painted in a red livery very similar to that of London Transport trolleybuses, even to the narrow cream band at the lower edge of the upper deck main panels. This time the chassis type was 9612E, signifying fluid flywheel and pre-selective transmission. Huddersfield requested metal-framed bodies, but agreed to accept composite construction as NCB promised that delivery, subject to the receipt of the chassis, would be made in August 1948. The price was £1,895 each for the bodies, but they were not completed until mid-1949.

Despite the severe shortage of raw materials, which were controlled by the Ministry of Supply, production in 1946 and 1947 at NCB was running at an average of three complete buses every week. This was quite an achievement for a company that had built less than 90 coaches and buses in the years before 1940. Production was running flat out in late February 1947 when a crisis arose.

The wartime Guy chassis was originally designed with the Gardner 5LW engine, but in order to accommodate the more powerful 6LW version, it was necessary to add 4½in (115mm.) to the bonnet length. The Government was persuaded by Guy to allow this extra length to be added to the 26ft 0in legal maximum length of the bus, rather than reduce the available lower deck passenger space. An emergency regulation (in Government terms, a 'Statutory Instrument') was approved in 1942 to permit this, and from 1943 all Guy chassis had the long bonnet, notwithstanding which engine was fitted. The wheelbase remained the same, the extra length being at the front end. The original short wartime version was later identified by enthusiasts as the Guy Arab Mark I, and the longer version as Mark II.

All the material for the framework and panels had been allocated and cut for a batch of ten Guy Arabs for Northern General, due for delivery in May 1947. Assembly had just been started when it was realised that the sanction for the extra length would finish at the end of April 1947, after which the bodies would be too long to meet the re-instated 26ft 0in maximum length under the Construction and Use Regulations. There was then the most tremendous panic, because unless the buses were completed, certified and taxed before this date, they would be unusable. It would have been necessary to machine new shorter longitudinal body members, not to mention the new length window pans and many other items. The cost to recover the situation would have been tremendous, even if permits could have been obtained to buy the replacement wood. The work was finished in time, but the paint was barely dry on the last bus! The vehicles concerned were NGT Nos. 1207-1216 (ACN 507-516), and the irony of the situation was that Northern never used 6LW engines in their Guy buses.

An order for 15 Guy Arabs for Yorkshire Woollen District, another BET company, followed this near disaster, this time to the new short length. The changed length of the Guy chassis was achieved by simply removing 4½in from the end. While the interiors were very similar to the NGT buses, the

Facing page, upper: In 1947 Bradford took delivery of a batch of 20 NCB bodies on the provincial version of the AEC 'RT' chassis. They were amongst the first post-war non-utility Bradford buses, and delivery took place between December 1947 and March 1948. *(Turner's [Photography] Ltd)*

Facing page, lower: The Huddersfield lowbridge buses were on AEC 9612E chassis, denoting the refined pre-selector/fluid flywheel version. Note the trafficator (direction indicator) on the front bulkhead. *(Turner's [Photography] Ltd)*

exteriors were to a very sombre, if smart, dark red livery relieved with three cream bands. Clayton front destination and route number boxes were fitted. Unlike NGT, Yorkshire Woollen used the larger Gardner 6LW engine in all their buses, necessary for the very steep hills around their home town of Dewsbury in the Yorkshire West Riding.

Cumberland Motor Services had received wartime NCB bodies on 15 Leyland chassis, and awarded NCB with an order for 25 lowbridge bodies on Leyland PD1 chassis. It is known that the Cumberland management was unhappy at delivery delays in this contract due, it is believed, to shortages of materials. The order was reduced to 20, and delivery of GAO 761-780 was spread between February 1948 and June 1949.

In May 1948 Northern Coachbuilders received a compliment from no less a figure than the Chancellor of the Exchequer, Sir Stafford Cripps. He quoted NCB as an example of how increased production could be achieved by a spirit of co-operation throughout the factory. At a press conference he said, "With very little increase in the labour force and despite material shortages, Northern Coachbuilders has doubled their 1946 output during 1947." NCB publicity at this time quoted a weekly output of eight to ten bodies, though the authors found the average to be less than half this figure, as mentioned earlier.

The late 1940's were in many respects good years for both transport operators and the manufacturing industry that supplied it. Despite shortages of materials and skilled labour, many firms who had not previously built bus bodywork found a ready market for their products. If the idea that there was a shortage of skilled labour sounds odd, remember that for six years of war few new apprentices had been trained, consequently, there was a large gap in the available number of skilled coachbuilders. The Government initiated a scheme whereby returning servicemen who had not previously had a trade could be given places in industry. These people, who became known as 'dilutees', would in time become very useful but, like apprentices, it took several years for them to complete their training. Many of them went on to very successful careers afterwards.

Yorkshire Woollen District was another **BET** operator to try **NCB** bodywork, in this case only one batch of 15 on **Guy Arab** chassis with the long **Gardner 6LW** engine. They were noticeable for their prominent 'Clayton' indicator and route number boxes. All the **BET** red liveried fleets were different in shades, and the YWD dark purple-red lined out in gold was very attractive, as seen here on **No. 532 (HD 7817)**, ready for delivery in October 1947.
(Turner's [Photography] Ltd)

Cumberland Motor Services had received 15 wartime NCB bodies on Leyland chassis, and awarded NCB with a post-war order for lowbridge bodies on Leyland PD1 chassis. The delivery was spread between February 1948 and June 1949. Here GAO 780 from that delivery is seen before delivery to the operator when new.
(Turner's [Photography] Ltd)

Material shortages were a different story. The Government, through the Ministry of Supply, set up an allocation system, effectively rationing all the necessary raw materials. Far more serious though was the shortage of seasoned timber. Again due to the war, virtually no new hardwood had been cut for six years, because of the shortage of manpower and ,of course, imports had not been possible. Production of softwood, essential for the arms industry, had been maintained with the help of members of the Women's Timber Corps known as the 'Lumberjills', of which the full story has yet to be told.

Because timber is a living organism, it has to be 'seasoned' before it can be used for construction. This involves leaving the sawn wood to dry under cover from the rain, but open to the air for anything up to five years. A further spell of time is then spent drying it indoors, to accustom the material to its future in dry stable conditions. At Northern Coachbuilders, the preferred woods were ash for the pillars and oak for the crossbearers, and Columbian pine for cant rails and other non-load bearing sections.

Unfortunately, all seasoned timber had been used up long ago, and coachbuilders were forced to use 'green' timber. Various methods were adopted to cope with this, such as 'kiln' drying in ovens, and the use of chemical dips. Northern Coachbuilders was seriously affected by these shortages, which were exacerbated by the rigid bureaucratic control of supplies, and even with careful selection of what wood was available, found that some of it very quickly warped out of the shape that it had been machined into. By its very nature, such wood was difficult to detect, and the sort of device that is used today to determine the amount of moisture in timber was not available.

The Government allowed the import of a small amount of hardwood, including some with unfamiliar names and characteristics. Some of it was almost unworkable! The most successful of these imports was the 'African walnut' that was turned into some very attractive window finishers. Other examples, jacquitiba or lacquaruba were teak substitutes, and could be used in place of oak. The company never resorted to the use of softwood for any part of the load bearing structure, as some bodybuilders were reputed to have done. The big problem for the company was that none of this hardwood was properly seasoned.

Consequently, there were some horrific problems. With the worst of these, such as bowed and twisted pillars or waist rails, buses had to be returned from the operators, to be stripped down and the faulty wood replaced. Nevertheless, the numbers of such failures were no greater than other coachbuilders using composite construction, who were all affected to various degrees by this difficulty. Customer confidence in NCB remained high, as the company received a number of repeat orders.

Because the country was almost bankrupt due to the cost of the recently ended world war, the Government exhorted industry to do all in their power to export their products, to bring much-needed foreign currency back into Britain. Indeed, export quotas were laid down for some products, and these had to be met before permission was given for the purchase of certain raw materials. Thus, the NCB sales team obtained an export order for bus bodies to meet these requirements. It was for four standard double-deck bodies on Guy Arab chassis for the South Western Bus Company, Ceylon, now Sri Lanka.

In this case, the term 'standard' was somewhat misleading; while the appearance was normal, under the 'skin' they were quite different. For example, insulating material was fitted between the inner and outer roof panels, to reduce the temperature. Because of the climate in Ceylon and the presence of voracious termites, our native oak and ash could not be used for the structure. Teak was the only suitable wood, and this could only be acquired by obtaining a special licence from the Ministry of Supply. The company was only allowed to buy exactly the amount needed to build four bodies, and specially treated board was required for the floors.

Now the woodmill is a fairly dangerous place to work, and the one at NCB was no different. Accidents happened not only to people but to work in progress and to tools. A key item in the woodmill was a long wooden rule, used for marking out

Interestingly, to ensure that the Ceylon buses conformed to the UK Regulations, one of them was tested on the NCB tilt platform. Watching from the right is EG Peacock, Works Manager. On the opposite page two complete buses stand outside the works waiting to be taken to the docks by their delivery drivers.
(Senior Transport Archive)

the pieces of wood for cutting. A frequent occurrence was for the end of the rule to catch a fast revolving blade on a machine, thereby losing the end. The rule would then be deliberately cut at the one-foot mark, and marked to show this until a new rule could be obtained. 'Everybody knows' the foreman would shout above the din of the machines. That is, until the severely rationed supply of teak came in for the Ceylon bodies.

Yes, that's right, a large number of pieces of teak were cut exactly one foot short. The Ministry sent an official to the factory to measure the scrapped parts before another licence was granted for the replacement teak. The only NCB export order was severely delayed, and no more export orders for buses were completed, probably to the relief of everyone.

The Ceylon contract was divided between several bodybuilders including Leyland and, as here, Park Royal. The London factory doorway provides a great contrast with the scene in service. Double-deck buses would become commonplace in Ceylon as second-hand examples from the UK found their way there, especially former London Transport RTs. *(Senior Transport Archive)*

12 – Complication

The Single-Deckers

Single-deck buses and coaches had formed the major part of NCB passenger vehicle production before 1940. Many operators, therefore, expected NCB to resume manufacture of these as soon as the war ended. Sadly for them this never occurred, at least in the manner expected by the old customers. Though several designs were prepared in the drawing office, and the managing director was quoted in a press statement as saying that single-deckers were about to be built, it was found that there was insufficient space in the factory to introduce a new range of bodies. There is, however, some evidence that one coach body may have been built.

One of the aims of Malcolm Smith was that the standard double-deck body would be complemented with a luxury coach body. The authors have been told that to achieve this, one of the most experienced coachbuilders was given the task of building a prototype, probably at the Benfield Road site. The 29-seat body was constructed on trestles, and is said to have closely resembled the Duple Vista, at that time the market leader, to be found on several hundred Bedford OB chassis all over the country. When completed, there was no chassis available, as all were 'spoken for' by other established coachbuilders, and the body was covered in sheets of green tarpaulin. Eventually, it is said, a Bedford OB chassis was found, but it is not known if it was new or had been previously used. The completed coach is thought to have gone to the Appleby & Jordan (Bedlington) partnership by Dixon Jordan, at an unknown date. There were three Bedford OBs in the A & J fleet, though all were previously believed to have had 'genuine' Duple bodies. No further knowledge about this coach has come to light.

Because of the 'flow-line' production system referred to earlier, the manufacture of the components, sub-assemblies and assemblies for the standard double-deckers occupied the whole of the works. This enabled the company to achieve very fast turn-round of orders, at very competitive prices, and was one of the reasons for its success. To introduce another range in the same space would have seriously disrupted the smooth running of the operation. Indeed, this is what did happen, as will be explained.

It has been mentioned that before the war the chief engineer, Horace Hatton, had previously held a similar post at Brush Coachworks, Loughborough. Brush had historical links with the British Electric Traction group and, consequently, had built many bodies for them to their designs. These were known as BEF (British Electrical Federation) bodies and were built for BET by several other manufacturers as well as Brush. Therefore, it was not surprising that the BET approached NCB with the idea of placing orders for BEF bodies with them. This approach was potentially too good to reject, so that orders were accepted in 1947 for bodies on Leyland Tiger PS1 chassis, 19 for Yorkshire Traction and 10 for Stratford-upon-Avon Blue Motors.

When the drawings for these were received, it was found that the designs required a large number of different components to be manufactured. The designs and specifications had been in existence for a number of years, and several well-known coachbuilders had successfully built buses using them. The NCB production team found great difficulty in translating these drawings into hardware at first because additional detail drawings, jigs and tools that previous manufacturers had already produced for them, were necessary. It was decided to manufacture one set of components initially, to test the assembly work to ensure that everything was correct. The immediate effect was to slow down the main double-deck production while the parts were made. The next problem was to find space in the works to build the first bus, and suitable craftsmen to work on it.

Consequently, the new single-decker stood forlornly in a corner of the paint shop for many months, with only occasional work being done. A visiting inspector from the BEF, who was very particular to ensure that every item of the specification and drawings was fully complied with, oversaw the work. Not unusually, there were a number of things that had to be rectified to meet his satisfaction. Eventually sufficient confidence was achieved with the completion of the framework to enable the directors to authorise the laying down of the first sets of parts for manufacture early in 1948. By Easter 1948, the customer for the first batch, Yorkshire Traction, was desperate. They decided to accept the first vehicle, which became 780 (BHE 441) and transferred the remainder of their order – to Brush Coachworks!

Stratford Blue was satisfied to wait for its allocation of ten vehicles, and the first was received in September 1948, being number 43 (GUE 249). The deliveries to Stratford were not completed until January 1949. There was in fact considerable disruption to normal production as not only had time and space to be found to manufacture the bodies, but jigs and fixtures had to be built on which to assemble the main structures such as side frames and roofs. The whole exercise was an unhappy event for the company and represented the first loss of confidence in it by customers. The fact that other companies in the industry managed to build BEF bodies during this period without any significant problems did not go unnoticed.

Inevitably there were recriminations, and several key members of staff left during this period, they will be mentioned again later. No further attempts were made by the company to build anything other than the extremely standardised ranges of double-deck buses.

An example of the BEF standard single-decker, built in this case by Brush for Yorkshire Woollen District in 1948, being supplied to the operator in March of that year. By that time HW Hatton from Brush was at NCB and the problems NCB was to encounter with its BET contract to build vehicles for Stratford Blue and Yorkshire Traction had become all-too obvious. BEF style bodies to this design were built by Roe, Weymanns and Brush, amongst other coachbuilders, but the price was keen and profit margin would have been quite tight. (John A Senior)

The BEF designed single-deck bodywork on Leyland Tiger PS1 chassis for the Yorkshire Traction Co proved troublesome to build, and the only one completed, in mid-1948, was 780 (BHE 441). YTC specified separate 'Clayton' destination and route number boxes. The concrete 'dragons teeth' lining the road at the edge of Newcastle Town Moor were meant to inhibit tank movement should the German army have invaded. It is seen above in its official portrait and below, in service in Waterdale, Doncaster. The use of Clayton equipment gave a somewhat heavy appearance to the front end. *(Turner's [Photography] Ltd); Allan Condie Collection)*

In 1947, as explained, Yorkshire Traction, through **BET**, placed orders for 19 Federation bodies on Leyland chassis. They had also ordered 23 of the same style bodies from Weymanns of Addlestone, these becoming AHE 461-483 and delivered in 1947/8, following on immediately after 18 for Western Welsh of which CKG 832 is shown here. As also explained the **NCB** 'batch' became the single vehicle shown opposite after YTC cancelled the balance due to the unacceptable delay in completing the order. The residue of this order – 18 buses – was transferred to Brush. Weymanns built only 41 Federation bodies, in these two batches – had they had their fingers burned too?
(Senior Transport Archive)

By contrast the otherwise similar **BET**-designed bodies built by **NCB** for the **Stratford Blue Motors** fleet benefited from the neater destination arrangement, as can be seen above. They appeared to blend happily into the town's atmosphere and two of them, numbers 43 and 44, stand ready for their next departures in the view to the right. After the delay in the delivery of this order the company's next order for single-deckers went to **Willowbrook**, as can be seen over the page.
(Turner's [Photography] Ltd) ; David Harvey)

This advertisement below illustrates the Willowbrook body as supplied to several BET customers. It did not attempt to fully replicate the BEF design, but it did include a number of features required by the BET organisation. Stratford Blue's next single-deck Leylands were indeed supplied by Willowbrook, four of them as here to dual-purpose specification and two as buses.
(Senior Transport Archive)

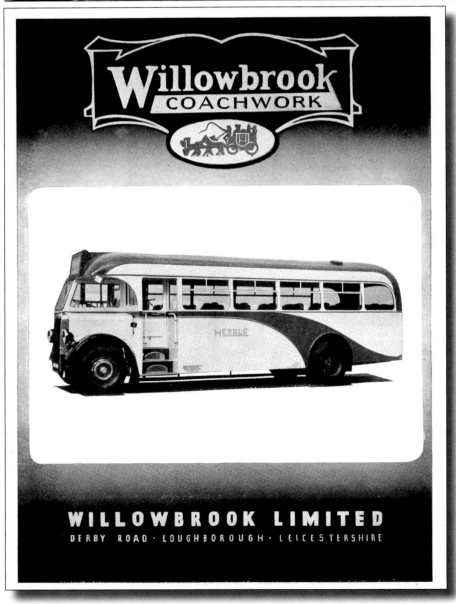

Facing page: A series of advertisements by NCB appeared in the trade press between 1939 and 1945. They concentrated on features of the body construction and the skills of the workforce. Malcolm Smith was prominent. The draughtsman in the top advertisement is Jack Herdman, seen again on page 141.
(Geoff Burrrows collection)

13 – Procession

More Double-Deckers

Meanwhile, going back to 1947, the production of the standard double-deck bodies continued, and orders continued to come in. Now that the Ministry of Supply system of vehicle allocation had ended, the company could be quietly satisfied that all their orders were being received on merit. Indeed, a number of customers placed repeat orders, including NGT, Newcastle, South Shields, Sheffield and Bradford.

The NGT orders were for more Guy Arabs, bringing a total of 50 standard NCB-bodied Guys to their fleet, in addition to the ten new AECs, the BMMO REDD and the first batch of five AEC re-bodies, including the prototype. The bodies for 20 outstanding Guys, numbered 1187-1206 (GUP 787-806) were correctly built to the revised short length, and delivered between December 1947 and March 1948. The final 10 (BCN 127-136) were sent to the operator in March 1949.

Newcastle bought 50 more trolleybus bodies, this time they were 56-seaters, similar to those supplied to Maidstone, Bradford and South Shields. They were mounted on 25 BUT 9611T chassis (LTN 554-578) and 25 Sunbeam F4 chassis (LTN 529-553), and in addition, 30 AEC Regent III motor buses (NBB 251-280). These were finished in the cadmium yellow livery previously restricted to the trolleybus fleet instead of the former navy blue motorbus livery. All the Newcastle trolleybuses and buses were fitted with four vertical body-lifting plates attached to the exterior edges of the bulkheads, a feature unique to Newcastle Corporation.

South Shields ordered ten bodies for mounting on Sunbeam chassis to serve the needs of their expanding trolleybus network. Though similar to the three already supplied, this time they incorporated many features required by the South Shields specification that had not been available on the previous orders, including 'Lace Web' seating and continuous bell push strips above the windows. The 'Pronto' bell pushes were made from polished wood designed to resemble the wood cappings used around the remainder of the window frames. CU 4873-4877 were delivered in August 1947 and CU 4943-4947 in 1948. A new feature was introduced by South Shields on these bodies, route number boxes were fitted at the front, though they were not used until 1950, by which time most of the existing fleet had been modified to suit.

Unlike the parent Northern General company, Tynemouth & District continued to favour AEC double-deckers after the war, and between 1946 and 1948 bought 29 Regent Mark II chassis with Weymann metal-framed bodies. The second of two batches ordered in 1946 was not delivered until 1948, and this late arrival may have been responsible for the temporary transfer of the ten NGT Guys with NCB bodies (ACN 507-516) to Tynemouth when nearly new in 1947. In May 1947 a further eight AEC Regent III chassis were ordered for the Tynemouth/Wakefields fleet, with Weymann metal-framed bodies. When they appeared in 1949 they carried standard NCB composite bodies similar to those in the parent Northern fleet (FT 6557-6564). Presumably Weymann was unable to meet the delivery date required by Tynemouth.

Glasgow Corporation gave NCB two good orders during this period, and Glasgow's first post-war AECs had NCB bodies; FYS 171-190 startled the workforce in the factory when they were first seen painted in their orange, green and cream colours. Delivery commenced in June 1948, by which date Glasgow had modified their livery from green roofs to cream. The first two were painted with green roofs, with the green extended over the rear dome to window ledge level, and the emergency door in cream. The next two were similar, but

Contemporaries of the Newcastle AEC Regents seen overleaf were eight in 1949 with conventional transmission for Tynemouth & Wakefields. They were much more unusual, however, as the Northern General Group did not standardise on the Regent III as it did with earlier Regents, and this batch were originally ordered with metal-frame Weymann bodies. The photograph in the upper view of the bus in North Shields heading down hill to the Ferry Terminal shows the original fully lined-out livery with large fleet names, made possible by the ommission of the waist panel mouldings. The first two carried the name of the associated 'Wakefield's' company as seen below. *(Roy Marshall; Geoff Burrows)*

In 1949 Newcastle took delivery of 25 Sunbeam F4s and 25 BUT 9611T two-axle trolleybuses with NCB 56-seat bodies. They were, apart from being shorter and obviously missing the third axle, very similar to the 30ft-long 70-seater Sunbeam S7s. One of the Sunbeams, number 553 (LTN 553) demonstrates a further difference between the two types, the concealed trolley gantry on the Sunbeams. The BUTs lacked this feature.
(Turner's [Photography] Ltd)

Newcastle Corporation also bought 30 AEC Regent III motor buses with NCB bodies in 1949. Now number 269 (NBB 269) takes the stand in the photographer's usual favoured spot. These were the first Newcastle motor buses to carry the yellow and cream 'trolleybus' livery. All previous motor buses for the Corporation were dark navy blue. *(Turner's [Photography] Ltd)*

NCB built a double-deck body for a Daimler CVD6 demonstrator in 1948. One of the first visits of GHP 259 was to Bournemouth, as seen here, during its tours of Britain and a trip to Denmark. The blue and silver livery was quite striking. As mentioned in the text it was sold to Northern Roadways of Glasgow in December 1948. For many years it was used for school and works contracts in Ayrshire, before being bought by Garelochhead Coach Services in 1952. As a concession to the Scottish climate in winter, it was fitted with platform doors by Gaerlochhead.
(David Stanier courtesy Garry Ward)

Newcastle trolleybus 563 (LTN 563) is seen outside Newcastle Central Station. The NCB body, mounted on a BUT 9611T chassis, illustrates the easily recognisable difference, having an exposed trolley gantry, unlike the Sunbeams. *(Alan Cross)*

The penultimate batch of motor buses delivered to Newcastle Corporation included number 269 (NBB 269). It is seen operating on service 8, the Spital Tongues circular, which passed the NCB factory in Claremont Road. *(RHG Simpson)*

with green emergency doors. The remainder, from FYS 175 onwards had the newly standardised cream roofs.

A further 20 buses were supplied to Glasgow in the following year. This time the chassis were Daimler CVD6s, and FYS 101-120 had identical bodies to the AEC's. One of the problems arising from meeting the Glasgow specification arose from the number of vertical stanchions (handpoles) called for in the lower deck. These all had to be bent into some very peculiar shapes in order to clear the many traps in the floor that were necessary to gain access to chassis equipment such as the gearbox. The livery was the same as that adopted for the later AECs.

Transport Vehicles (Daimler) Ltd, the full title of the famous chassis manufacturer, ordered a body from NCB in 1948. This was for a standard double-decker with no frills, mounted on a CVD6 chassis to be used as a demonstrator. Features of GHP 259 were a rectangular front destination indicator and a blue and silver livery. At this time there was an export promotional visit to Copenhagen, Denmark, by six Daimler double-deckers from various operators' fleets. It later visited many operators around Britain before being sold to Northern Roadways of Glasgow and then subsequently, in 1952, Garelochhead Coach Services in Dumbartonshire, Scotland. Despite the title, this was primarily a bus operator with a fleet of about ten double-deck buses and a lesser number of coaches.

The City of Oxford Motor Services ordered 25 lowbridge bodies for AEC Regent chassis, they were particularly handsome vehicles in their maroon, red and duck egg blue/green livery. They were fitted with Clayton destination boxes; these large rectangular boxes opened at the front to give access to a choice of four separate blinds, each on their own rollers. Registered MWL 980-993, NWL 709-718 and NFC 311, they were the first double-deck AEC chassis to combine the 9.6 litre engine with a manual gearbox and vacuum brakes. During the course of their manufacture, AEC introduced a new chassis designation system to enable the various types to be more readily identified.

The City of Oxford Motor Services ordered 25 lowbridge bodies for AEC Regent chassis. This operator specified gutter mouldings to be fitted above the windows instead of the usual rainshields. This subtly altered the appearance. *(Alan Cross)*

The 20 NCB-bodied AEC Regents supplied to Glasgow Corporation are represented here by A72 (FYS 172). They remained as part of the Glasgow fleet for many years, together with 20 of the similarly bodied Daimlers of which D5 is seen below in service. Note that the AEC carries a green-painted roof, as built, whilst the Daimler has the post-1948 cream version. Rain shields were only required over the opening windows by Glasgow.
(Turner's [Photography] Ltd); Senior Transport Archive/Roy Marshall)

Thus, the first five were type 0961, the remainder, though the specification was unchanged, received a new designation, 9612A. The new Oxford fleet was then seriously affected by the timber problems referred to earlier in this narrative. They were fitted with chains wrapped around the complete body for support to prevent further damage occurring during the journey from Oxford to Newcastle for repair. Following these repairs the buses went on to achieve 14 years satisfactory operation in the Oxford fleet.

The standard NCB body did not change materially during its five-year production run, though there were a number of detail changes. The windscreen and cab side windows became less angular, and a greater range of seat frames became available, to quote two examples. These and other improvements became possible as the problems of component suppliers eased, as more materials gradually became available again.

The company had noted that since the war many operators had simplified their liveries, and few now required the waist bands underneath the windows to be painted a different colour to that of the main panels. Hence the decision was taken to delete the waist moulding from the bodies, considerably reducing the number of parts required, as well as speeding up production. This simple change altered the appearance, giving a smoother finish. Cab design was also improved to reduce the number of corners and sharp angles.

A new staircase was developed, with one step fewer on the first stage from the platform. Compensation for this was by the addition of an extra step on the second stage, which projected slightly into the rear of the offside lower deck ceiling. This simple re-arrangement created much more space on the platform, and because there were now two turns on the staircase, made that safer, too. The design was very similar to the Roe safety staircase, but unlike it, there was no loss of seating over the offside wheelarch.

Because of the continuing problems concerning the supply of seasoned timber, many operators were now seriously interested in 'all metal' bodywork. Before the war, this had not been the most popular choice with smaller operators. There had been a determined campaign by supporters of composite bodywork to highlight the perceived difficulties in repairing accident damage on metal-framed bodies. In addition many manufacturers then lacked expertise in this type of work. The difference now was that many bodybuilders had been involved in aircraft manufacture during the war. The experience thus gained stood them in good stead when coachbuilding was subsequently resumed. Operators could now be confident that 'all metal' bodies would probably outlast the traditional composite designs. They also found that many servicemen returning to work for them had experienced work on airframe structures during the war, and were, therefore, able to work on and repair metal bodywork without difficulty. They could also look to the experience of the larger operators, whose metal bodies had in most cases stood up to the war years much better than their composite bodies.

Northern Coachbuilders design and development office did many calculations on the subject. As mentioned earlier, steel bodies had been proposed for post war production, but that line of development was not pursued. Aluminium alloy structures were considered now that the supply situation was easier, and eventually one alloy framed top deck was built, to be mounted on a normal composite lower deck. The structure was built using aluminium angles, instead of the originally envisaged extrusion of a similar section to the steel design patented in 1947. The exterior appearance was identical to a standard body, with only minor differences inside. The bus became Northern General Guy Arab 1236 (BCN 136), numerically the last 7ft 6in wide NCB body for that operator. It took to the road in April 1949. Unfortunately, after only eleven years service, 1236 was involved in a serious accident and written off.

By this time, a much more radical change was about to be made. Since 1946, 8ft 0in wide vehicles had been legally acceptable on specified routes and it was becoming clear that before long the 7ft 6in wide bus would be obsolescent. As

The manufacture of specialised stock of bespoke sections for bus construction was big business and Tube Investments (TI) owned several subsidiaries, including MetSec as here. They would work with the bodybuilders, producing sections to their patented specification ensuring that other patents were not infringed. Freddy Rayer, mentioned on page 143, had been recruited from Brush to become the TI panjandrum in this area. (Senior Transport Archive)

Although Maidstone Corporation placed no more orders from NCB, as mentioned in the text, Maidstone's last trolleybus, number 72 (HKR 11) survived into preservation and is seen operating at the Trolleybus Museum at Sandtoft. *(David Cole)*

John Hardy Herdman, Chief Draughtsman, left in late 1947, going to Barnards in Norwich with Horace Hatton. Herdman later moved to South Africa, reaching the height of his career there as recorded in Chapter 16.

was mentioned earlier, an order from Maidstone Corporation was lost because no 8ft 0in body was available. The NCB design and development office looked at ways in which it may have been possible to widen the standard body. The original intention was to retain the same shape, and to simply add six inches to the width. The problem with that idea was the roof.

The lightweight NCB roof had been giving problems ever since its adoption. At certain speeds, the vibration caused loud drumming noises, giving the same effect as shaking a large flat metal panel. Trolleybuses were not affected, as the steel trolley gantry gave rigidity to the upper deck sides and this added sufficient stiffness to the roof to prevent this. Those buses fitted with interior stanchions in the upper saloon were also immune as these acted as stiffeners, but most operators preferred to keep the upper deck uncluttered.

Because a larger area has a greater tendency to vibrate, it was clear that if the same design for the roof structure was employed on a wider vehicle, the 'biscuit tin lid' effect would be even worse. Therefore, it was obvious that a complete re-design of the roof for an 8ft 0in wide body would be required. This would not have been difficult, and could have been achieved by introducing a stronger framework. Hatton was unwilling to compromise, and the problem was still unresolved when he and several other senior members of staff left the company. This was due partly to the repercussions following the single-deck debacle described on page 129. These included Richard Booth, production director who left in April 1947, and Jack Herdman, chief draughtsman who went to Barnards to join Hatton when the latter left in November 1947. Hatton would later become production manager at East Lancashire Coachbuilders in Blackburn in April 1950. After several short-term moves Herdman moved to Weymanns, and was then appointed to its subsidiary Bus Bodies (SA) Pty in South Africa in 1947, where he later became Managing Director.

14 – Succession

A New Start

Following the departure of Messrs Hatton, Herdman, Booth *et al*, by early 1948, Malcolm Smith invited Bill Bramham to join the company as Director and General Manager. Bramham had begun his career with an apprenticeship shared between Clayton Sons and Hercules Engineering. After war service in WW1 he returned to Hercules, leaving them as assistant chief draughtsman to join Charles Roe, the well-known Leeds coachbuilders as chief draughtsman in 1926. In 1936 he became General Manager of Eastern Coach Works Ltd in Lowestoft when that company was formed from Eastern Counties Omnibus Company. He was responsible for ECW's late 1930's designs, and the double-deckers bore a close resemblance to Roe bodywork. In 1943 the aircraft manufacturer Short Bros of Rochester in Kent, famous for their Sunderland flying boats, found itself in difficulties. The Ministry of Aircraft Production was seriously concerned about this, and replaced the board of directors with their own nominees. Sir Frederick Heaton, Chairman of the Tilling group of bus companies, was appointed Chairman, and Bramham was seconded to the company, becoming one of the directors. As one of three full time officials, he was responsible for ensuring that production met the urgent needs of the armed forces.

After returning to ECW as Director and General Manager, his greatest achievements were his wartime ECW designs that were to become classics as they developed through the early post-war period, notable for well-balanced design, and extremely sound structure. Indeed, the continuity of this shape and construction could be discerned in all double-deck ECW bodies built until the end of Bristol Lodekka production in 1980.

Bramham's arrival at Northern Coachbuilders was part of a series of events which, taken together, would greatly influence the future of not only NCB but many other coachbuilders. It is appropriate, therefore, to consider what influenced him to leave Eastern Coach Works, and others to leave Brush to join him. ECW was part of the giant Tilling Group which had just been nationalised, and, as recorded elsewhere, would in future be able to sell its products only to that group's constituent companies. ECW's presence at the 1948 Motor Show must have a great embarrassment since it was unable to take any orders, its future production being planned and then organised at the former Tilling headquarters.

It would have been obvious to Bramham that many of his former contacts outside the group would have been potential customers for the bodies he had designed, and for which he held some patents. These bodies had already been fitted to Leyland Titan and Guy Arab chassis, with which the Claremont Road staff were very familiar. Clearly Malcolm Smith also recognised this when inviting Bramham to join NCB, and a new management team was appointed under his guidance. Most important of these was SN Churchill, who became Works Manager. Coincidentally, Churchill was another former Brush Coachworks staff member, having been Chief Draughtsman and Designer between 1943 and 1946, before taking an appointment at Charles Roberts of Wakefield, builders of railway rolling stock, buses and trams. He had been apprenticed at Harringtons. To complete the reorganisation, in 1948 the battery-electric division became Smith's Electric Vehicles Ltd, another autonomous company in the Ringtons group, based in the Team Valley Trading Estate, Gateshead. Horace W Heyman was appointed Managing Director of the new company.

Before long Brush would cease to build bus and coach bodywork and the two men may have had knowledge of this. Although unconnected with the Newcastle story Brush also lost their metal-framing specialist when Freddy Rayer, who had designed the original Metro-Cammell bodywork way back in the

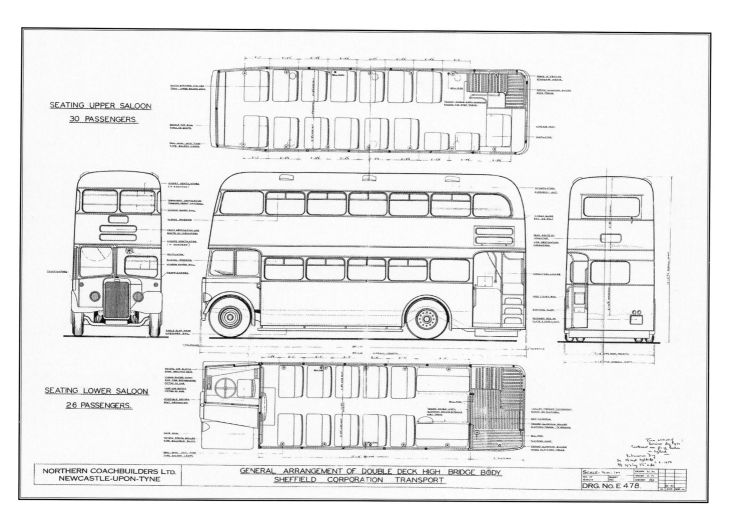

SEATING UPPER SALOON
30 PASSENGERS

SEATING LOWER SALOON
26 PASSENGERS.

NORTHERN COACHBUILDERS LTD.
NEWCASTLE-UPON-TYNE

GENERAL ARRANGEMENT OF DOUBLE DECK HIGH BRIDGE BODY
SHEFFIELD CORPORATION TRANSPORT

DRG. No. E 478.

This is the tender drawing produced by NCB for the proposed bodies to be fitted to Leyland PD2 chassis for Sheffield. In drawing form, the design is even more similar to the original ECW version. *(Courtesy Sheffield Transport Study Group)*

1920s, had also just left Brush to joint Tube Investments, owners of Accles & Pollock from whom NCB may have bought metal sections for body construction.

Bramham's first task at NCB was to produce an 8ft 0in wide double-deck body. Since he obviously took great pride in what he had done at ECW, it was perhaps inevitable that the new bodies looked like those from Eastern Coach Works. The construction owed nothing to previous NCB designs, indeed certain features that had been patented jointly by Bramham and his former employers closely resembled those that could be found on the new NCB designs.

The construction of the 'Bramham' bodies incorporated a structure called 'continuous rail'; similar to one that had been patented by ECW and Bramham. This patent stated that the longitudinal members of the body structure passed through slots in the pillars before being secured, which gave great strength to the side frames. It is noteworthy that the Roe patented waistrail, which gave great strength to their bodywork, was similarly designed. In their case, it was a visible identification feature, and protruded slightly along the sides of their buses. At NCB the continuous aluminium waistrails were slotted through the wood pillars on both decks.

The ECW method of composite construction was used for this new range of bodies; it was well respected and the Lowestoft company had already built several hundred. The NCB designs were intended to be as close as practicable to the original versions. Reputedly, Bramham would lean over the draughtsman's shoulder, point and say 'That isn't close enough to the ECW design, change it!'

Another feature used on the new bodies was a new type of glazing, with radii on all corners of the windows, with little intrusion inside the body. It is

believed that one of the 'standard' 7ft 6in wide NCB bodies was fitted with this style of glazing as a trial. There is no further record of which vehicle was used, and it may have been removed and replaced by the usual 'Widney' glazing before leaving the factory.

Nevertheless, even ECW had been having problems with unseasoned timber, and quite a number of their bodies had to be replaced within a very few years. That company had already begun the development of metal-framed bodies, and the designs were well advanced when Bramham left to join NCB. So it was not unexpected to find reference to steel-framed bodies in items of correspondence that have come to light. It can be safely assumed that Bramham only intended to use composite construction until his metal-framed designs were complete, and as soon as supplies of steel and aluminium could be assured.

Further evidence of this lies in the five bay body design produced at Claremont Road. Eastern Coach Works had only produced one batch of this 8ft 0in highbridge version for Middlesbrough on Leyland PD1 chassis, before their four bay aluminium framed body was introduced, though a few buses were rebodied with the five bay version at a later date. It is interesting to note that more NCB bodies of this five bay, 8ft 0in wide highbridge type were built on new chassis than by ECW.

Northern General was the first customer, with 17 on Guy Arab chassis. Delivery began in April 1950, but their requirements were changed and the last six were diverted

Standing proudly in Claremont Road for the official photographs, 311 (NVK 311) was the first 'Bramham' body for Newcastle. The only visible clue that this was not an ECW body was the lack of 'push-out' front window ventilators. *(Turner's [Photography] Ltd)*

(Lower) Saved for posterity by preservationists, Newcastle 341 is seen here attending a rally. Beautifully restored, this rear view illustrates the clean lines of the ECW/NCB design. *(Senior Transport Archive)*

to the associated Gateshead Omnibus Company in June 1950, to be used for tram replacement. BCN 821-826 went to Gateshead, while BCN 877-887 went to the parent NGT. They were all identical buses, with NGT layout for destination and number blinds, but while the Northern versions were in their famous red livery, the Gateshead buses were in the tram derived maroon. Both, however, showed 'Shop at Binns' advertisements!

Once again Newcastle Corporation was the best customer, taking 40 of the new design (NVK 311-350) mounted on AEC 9612A chassis (ie with clutch and manual gearbox), which many observers thought a backward step from the previous pre-selective gearboxes. They were delivered between July and November 1950.

The most interesting order for the new body came from Cleethorpes, for GFU 692-695, mounted on BUT 9611T two-axle trolleybus chassis. Although ECW had never built any trolleybus bodies, here was an example of what they may have looked like had they done so. Unfortunately, they seemed to lack the elegance of the bus bodies, being very box-like in their cab and windscreen design.

These trolleybuses had a very interesting 'afterlife'. When the trolleybus system in Cleethorpes and Grimsby closed in 1960, they were sold to Walsall

"This is one I built earlier" as the saying goes! A genuine **ECW**-bodied Braham-designed **AEC** Regent operating in its home town of Lowestoft for the local operator. The similarity to the later Newcastle version from **NCB**, opposite, really needs no further comment.
(Senior Transport Archive)

Eastern Coach Works started work on what would become its standard highbridge post-war body during the war, by special government dispensation. When the Tilling Group became nationalised in 1948 it became one of the standard Tilling designs, seen throughout the country. From that time, however, it was only to be available to fleets in the Group, except where outstanding orders were being fulfilled. It appeared in lowbridge and highbridge form, in two widths – 7ft 6in and 8ft – and two lengths – 26ft and 27ft 6in. The Tynemouth vehicle, a 1938 rebodied Leyland Titan, shows the shorter and narrower version. Middlesbrough took Leyland PD1s with the wider version, below, and then Guys as seen opposite. When Bramham left to go to NCB this was the version he took with him. Just what his successor at Lowestoft, Bill Shirley, had to say about this seems not to have been recorded. *(Senior Transport Archive)*

This 'real' Eastern Coach Works-bodied Leyland PD1 in the Middlesbrough Corporation fleet shows how closely the NCB version replicated it. *(Geoff Burrows)*

The last **NCB** bodies for the Northern General group were 17 of the 8ft 0in wide version on Guy Arab chassis, represented in this photograph by No. 1387 (BCN 887). Only 11 entered service directly with Northern, in April and May of 1950. Because of a vehicle shortage in the tram conversion programme, the other six were painted in the livery of Gateshead & District to become the only NCB bodies in that fleet. They were sound and comfortable vehicles, but somewhat ponderous at their 7tons 18cwt weight, with only a Gardner 5LW engine to propel them up the steep Durham hills. This 1950 Guy Arab shows just how close the **NCB** version was to the **ECW** original at the foot of the page opposite. If Bramham had left **ECW** because he felt his future was bound to be restricted to following Tilling directives, and losing the ability to exercise his individuality, he had made certain that he could offer exactly what he believed his customers wanted. Yet some would continue to take the traditional **NCB** body. *(GoAhead)*

Middlesbrough Corporation bought a second batch of post-war ECW bodies, this time on Guy Arab chassis. This 'Pullman' version of the body, with four bays and deep windows, shows the direction that the ECW designers were moving towards when the Bristol Lodekka was conceived. *(Senior Transport Archive)*

Corporation Transport. Once there, three of them were drastically rebuilt, lengthened to 30ft 0in long with forward-entrances. The seating capacity went up from 54 to 69, and the staircase was simply moved forward, giving an unusual layout at the front of the lower deck. The name of the general manager at Walsall should sound familiar, none other than RE Cox! As a result, these became the last NCB trolleybuses to run in service, not being withdrawn until 1970, and probably the last operational NCB vehicles in Great Britain.

It is also believed that Bramham was preparing to introduce a single-deck body, similar (if not identical!) to the ECW body as fitted to the Bristol L series of chassis. This was another model Bramham could expect to sell well into his former customer's fleets until such time as the forthcoming underfloor-engined chassis came on the market. That it was not introduced is not surprising as, in addition to the factory capacity problems already mentioned, he would have wanted to go straight into metal-framed production when that became possible. There was also lurking in the background the imminent introduction of underfloor-engined single-deck chassis as mentioned, threatening to render conventional buses redundant overnight. He was avoiding committing NCB to what would, in effect, have been a short-lived product.

Bill Bramham also paid close attention to the production facilities. Before his arrival, the body shop was laid out so that three lines of buses followed each other around until they entered the finishing and paint shop. This meant that every day several man-hours were spent moving partly built vehicles forward to make way for new ones. As there were no batteries fitted during construction, this meant pushing! Bramham re-arranged the shop so that the vehicles were parked in echelon, that is, herringbone style. No more daily pushes! Another Bramham innovation was to identify each chassis on arrival by clearly painting the number and the customer's name on the front dash.

Facing page: **Cleethorpes Corporation** received the only four 8ft 0in wide **NCB** bodied trolleybuses to be built, mounted on **BUT 9611T** chassis. The livery of No. 62 (GFU 695) was unusual, but to the authors the overall effect was rather insipid, as seen in the top photograph taken in Claremont Road. The neat faring of the trolley gantry was a satisfactory feature, but the design of the driver's cab lacked inspiration. When the Grimsby and Cleethorpes undertakings were merged, a new blue and cream livery gave a slight improvement, as seen in the lower picture. However, by continuing the dark roof colour onto the rain shields, a 'frowning' attitude was introduced. Nevertheless, they were well built and long-lived bodies, and after the closure of the Grimsby-Cleethorpes trolleybus system in 1960 they went on to serve in Walsall until the closure of that system in 1970. *(Turner's [Photography] Ltd, Michael Dryhurst)*

If Bramham had indeed had ideas about producing a single-decker to fill the gap left by **ECW** supplying only Tilling fleets, then this would have been it. And North Western, staunch supporters of Lowestoft-designed buses, could well have been a potential customer. Though they had never purchased **NCB** bodywork, it is believed that **North Western** may have intended to buy some of their buses with 'Bramham' bodies from **NCB**. The single-deckers would have been similar to this early ECW version. They later placed a contract to rebody wartime Guy and pre-war Bristol double-deckers, although sadly in the event **NCB** were not able to fulfill their commitment as recorded on page 154. *(Senior Transport Archive)*

15 – Completion

A Sudden Shock

The battery-electric business was clearly thriving, and in order to be put in a secure position financially, became an autonomous company early in 1949, under the name of Smiths Electric Vehicles Ltd. The tenure of a 25,000 square foot factory at Princes Way, Team Valley, was obtained, where all production was then moved. The former factory in the Nissen huts was retained for storage. The Managing Director of the new company was Horace William Heyman, as recorded earlier, and the other directors, Douglas Smith, Snr and Douglas Smith, Jnr, retained the link with the Ringtons group. From this time onward there was no further involvement with Claremont Road, other than when vehicles were sent there for special signwriting.

This was not the first time that the Princes Way factory had been connected with the motor industry. Holland Coachcraft Ltd occupied the premises from 1937 until 1940, when many commercial vehicle bodies of modern design were built. One design in particular brought them to the notice of the general public, an aggressively streamlined laundry van, used by Meccano as a basis for its 'streamline bus' Dinky Toy model. Holland also built bodies for battery-electric vehicles! After Holland closed in 1940, the engineering manufacturer Sigmund Pumps moved into the factory and produced parts for Bren guns. The factory stood empty for some time after the war ended before Smiths took it over.

The development of the battery-electric business by NCB had been dramatic, in addition to supplying BEVs all over Great Britain, the company exported large numbers to many overseas countries, including Belgium, Canada, Denmark and New Zealand. At this point, the battery-electric production becomes a history in its own right, and the authors are leaving it for others to chronicle at some future time. There is also much more to be told about the early days of that enterprise, and will no doubt be written in due course.

Things now appeared to be very promising for the future of NCB at Claremont Road. A number of potential customers showed interest in the new 8ft 0in bodies and several previous customers were looking seriously at the new designs. Fortune had decided otherwise, however.

Sam Smith, OBE, JP, the founder and Chairman of Ringtons Ltd, Smiths Electric Vehicles Ltd, Cut-Out (Cartons) Ltd and Northern Coachbuilders Ltd, died on the 12th of August 1949 at the age of 77. Shortly afterwards the family received a demand from the Inland Revenue for a considerable sum to be paid in Death Duties. It was apparent that the financial health of the companies would be seriously affected if this money was paid out of capital. After due deliberation it was decided that the core business, Ringtons tea blending and distribution, should remain intact, together with Cut-Out (Cartons) Ltd, without which the tea could not be packaged. As already explained, the battery-electric vehicle business had been financially separated and re-structured as Smiths Electric Vehicles Ltd, and was, therefore, not affected. This left NCB which, whilst it appeared to have excellent prospects, was in all probability struggling to maintain enough business to remain viable.

The directors reluctantly decided that Claremont Road factory would have to close and the site sold to recoup the sum required for the Death Duties. The company would remain in existence, but on a vastly reduced scale, working from the facility in Benfield Road, Newcastle. The intention

N.C.B. Reorganisations

NORTHERN COACHBUILDERS, LIMITED, Newcastle-on-Tyne, has separated the public service vehicle and battery electric vehicle departments of its business. The battery electric department has been transferred to Smith's Electric Vehicles, Limited, of which the directors will be Mr. Douglas Smith, senior, Mr. Douglas Smith, junior, and Mr. H. W. Heyman. The latter will continue to manage the business and will hold the office of managing director. The public service vehicle department will be operated by Northern Coachbuilders, Limited, as hitherto and there will be no change in the ownership of the group as a whole. This division of interest coincides with a move by Smith's Electric Vehicles, Limited, into larger and more convenient premises at Princesway, Team Valley, Gateshead-on-Tyne, 11, where the full range of N.C.B. electric vehicles will be manufactured, including bodybuilding for all delivery trades and painting operations.

We regret to record the death of Mr. Sam Smith, O.B.E., J.P., chairman of Ringtons, Limited, of Newcastle-on-Tyne, and the subsidiary companies, Northern Coachbuilders, Limited, and Smith's Electric Vehicles, Limited. Mr. Smith, who was 77, was a Yorkshireman and began work in Leeds as an errand boy at the age of nine. He served a further 20 years with a Leeds firm before launching out on his own in Newcastle-on-

The late Mr. Sam Smith

Tyne and becoming in subsequent years the leading tea merchant of the area. The Ringtons fleet of horse-drawn vans for house-to-house tea delivery became a distinctive feature of the North East and, through the company's own coachbuilding department, led to the establishment of Northern Coachbuilders, Limited, in 1933, as a contribution to the need for new light industries on Tyneside. As recently recorded, the P.S.V. coachbuilding and battery electric vehicle departments of N.C.B. have been separated; Smith's Electric Vehicles, Limited., now operates a factory in the Team Valley trading estate, Gateshead.

Future of Northern Coachbuilders Ltd.

CLAREMONT ROAD WORKS SOLD TO MEET DEATH DUTIES

The way in which taxation, in the form of death duties, can cause a prosperous firm to close down, thereby creating considerable unemployment, is vividly revealed by a statement issued by Northern Coachbuilders Ltd., the well-known Newcastle body building firm. It reads as follows :—

Statement by Northern Coachbuilders Ltd.—Following the decease of Mr. Samuel Smith, O.B.E., J.P., founder of this Company, it has become necessary to conserve finance and to raise monies to meet substantial death duty liabilities. It is deeply regretted by the Company that, as a result, the necessity to sell its valuable freehold premises at Claremont Road, Newcastle upon Tyne, 2, has been forced upon it.

The future of the Company is not finally decided, but it is hoped that production may continue elsewhere on a modified basis.

Concurrently, the following statement was also issued :—

Statement by the Newcastle upon Tyne Co-operative Society Limited.—It has just been announced that the Newcastle upon Tyne Co-operative Society Limited have acquired the property at present occupied by Northern Coachbuilders Limited in Claremont Road, Newcastle upon Tyne. The buildings, which were erected between 1936 and 1940, have an area of 8,100 square yards or thereabouts and are one of the finest factory premises in the North of England. It is understood that the Newcastle upon Tyne Co-operative Society Limited intend to use the premises as a garage for their vehicles, joinery workshops, etc. The sale has been negotiated by Sanderson Townend & Gilbert, Chartered Surveyors and Estate Agents of this City.

was to continue the repair and painting of commercial vehicles, employing those members of staff who wished to stay with the company. Another small firm in the Ringtons portfolio, Lees Bakeries of Benton was also sold for the same reason.

With the benefit of hindsight, this move probably saved the company from a slow and undignified demise, as the tremendous demand for new buses after the war was already diminishing. Operators were either returning to their traditional suppliers, or to firms such as Leyland, that was now in a position to supply complete buses of exceptionally high standard with very quick delivery. During the next decade many well-known and respected coachbuilders and nearly all the newcomers to the industry were forced to close.

Having joined NCB in 1948 with high hopes, Bill Bramham was now in the embarrassing position of having to turn away orders for bus bodies. Several operators have been mentioned to the authors in this respect, without confirmation, but there is positive proof regarding Sheffield, where a tender from NCB had been accepted for 7ft 6in wide metal framed bodies on ten Leyland PD2 chassis as per the drawing on page 143. Bramham wrote to Sheffield in May 1950 declining the order, with great regret. The opportunity for NCB to build on the leading double-deck chassis of the period was also lost.

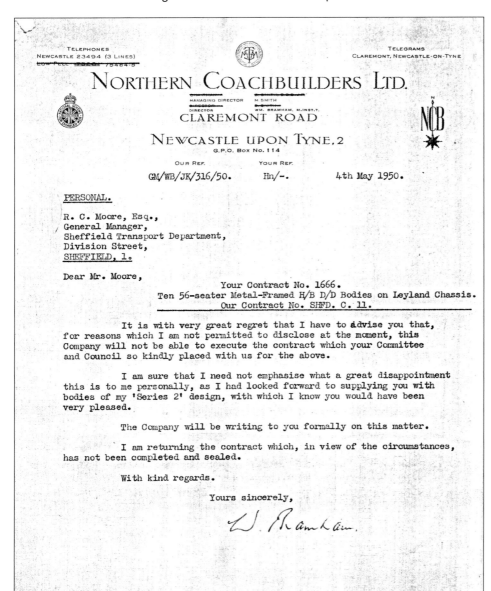

(Courtesy Paul Fox)

Teething problems! A new **Guy Arab** with one of the first 8ft 0in wide **NCB** bodies is standing near the Newcastle (Worswick Street) bus station, being considered by a puzzled-looking Northern General fitter. In June 1950, when this photograph was taken, these buses were initially used on the long Newcastle-Darlington service. *(Alan Cross)*

In the early 1950s these Willowbrook bodies were supplied to North Western on the pre-war Bristol chassis that may have been intended to receive NCB lowbridge 'Bramham' bodies. On the right is shown a wartime Guy Arab with a similar replacement body. This was perhaps not the most elegant design from Willowbrook. *(Senior Transport Archive both)*

Burton upon Trent Corporation had placed an order for six highbridge NCB bodies on Guy Arab chassis in 1947, but the chassis were not available until 1949. Burton then amended the order to a requirement for lowbridge bodies. The order was returned by NCB, and the bodies were supplied to Burton in 1950 by DJ Davies of Treforest, south Wales. A second trolleybus order for Cleethorpes, and one for full fronted forward-entrance double-deck Guy Arabs and double-deckers on Bristol chassis for India, were all declined, due to the impending closure of the company.

Northampton Corporation had placed a second order as early as September 1946. There would have been ten Daimler CVG6s, but the chassis were not available until 1949. Northampton was then unable to obtain authority for the loan necessary to buy them. Agreement for the cancellation of the order was reached with the NCB solicitors in 1951, a somewhat academic exercise, because coachwork construction had already ended.

Another outstanding order that was reluctantly surrendered was for the North Western Road Car Co, a BET company based at Stockport, Cheshire. This fleet had standardised on Bristol chassis from the 1930's, and many were giving such good service that it was decided to have them rebodied. Work was already in progress in late 1949 on the single-deckers in the fleet, and now it was the turn of the double-deckers. This was at the time when ECW, their preferred supplier, was prohibited from taking new orders from non-BTC companies. It is believed that orders may have been placed for all 64 of their 1938/39/40 Bristol K5G chassis to be fitted with new NCB bodies. They would have been the first NCB lowbridge double-deckers to the new designs. North Western also intended to fit the Bristol 'PV2' low-height radiators to the re-bodied chassis. Eventually Willowbrook Coachbuilders of Loughborough did the job, though the radiators weren't changed, either.

Sheffield became one of the final NCB customers, receiving a batch of ten 7ft 6in wide bodies of the old 'standard' design mounted on AEC 9621E chassis (MWA 825-834) in 1950. They had the normal Sheffield indicator layout, with the route number blind placed centrally above the destination. The last of these buses was not withdrawn from service until 1966, after years of satisfactory use.

Other orders delivered in that last full year of production were the 25 Sunbeam F4 trolleybuses for Newcastle (LTN 529-553), and ten similar vehicles for South Shields, also on Sunbeam F4 chassis. Four were delivered in August (CU 5100-5105) and six in October (CU 5279-5282), the final 7ft 6in wide NCB trolleybuses to be built. These two later orders revealed a detail

When the Grimsby-Cleethorpes trolleybus system closed in 1960, the NCB-bodied trolleybuses were sold to Walsall. Once there, three of them were drastically rebuilt, lengthened to 30ft, fitted with forward-entrance, and the existing staircase moved forward. The Walsall livery was even less attractive than those of the previous owners.
(Michael Dryhurst)

difference, which was to be found in the trolley gantries. These were now concealed under panelling, and because of this, the Newcastle Sunbeams could be easily identified. The Newcastle trolleybuses also had longer than normal trolleybooms, to prevent drips from the trolleyheads from falling onto the rear dome and staining the paint. The 8ft 0in wide AEC's for Newcastle have already been mentioned, the last left the works in November 1950, and was the penultimate delivery.

Sheffield became one of the final **NCB** customers, receiving a batch of ten bodies of the old 'standard' design mounted on **AEC 9621E** chassis in 1950. This time they had the normal Sheffield indicator layout, with the route number blind placed centrally above the destination. The last of these buses was not withdrawn from service until 1966. One of the city's many trams passes in the background. *(Alan Cross)*

South Shields received ten Sunbeam F4 trolleybuses with concealed trolley gantries in 1950. As with the Newcastle trolleybuses, the waist mouldings would have been superfluous and were omitted. Post-war shop buildings have risen from the rubble of the wartime blitz in the Market Place. *(Michael Dryhurst)*

16 – Conclusion

Close Down

By Christmas 1950 the factory was almost empty. Most of the employees had moved to other jobs, and all the outstanding orders except one had been completed. By coincidence, the final order to be completed by NCB was not for the new 8ft 0in wide bodies, but for ten Daimler CVG6s with 7ft 6in wide bodies for one of the first customers for the post war bodies, Aberdeen. Because of the general run down in the works, they were not completed until March 1951.

Unfortunately, these were amongst the shortest-lived NCB bodies, as they were all scrapped in 1960, and Alexanders re-bodied the chassis. It has to be surmised that most of the experienced staff had left NCB when they were built, resulting in unsatisfactory construction. The earlier batch from 1947 remained in service for longer, the last being withdrawn in 1963. This was despite a decision by Aberdeen Corporation in the mid-1950s not to spend any money rebuilding them, as they were then considered to be too far-gone. Instead, Aberdeen rebuilt a batch of utility Duple-bodied Daimlers dating from 1945, outliving the 1947 NCB Daimlers by two or three years.

Following the completion of this work, the remaining workforce and some of the machinery and equipment was taken to the Benfield Road premises. The items left in the Claremont Road factory were sold by auction in 1951, and later the Co-operative Wholesale Society bought the premises. Nearly all evidence of the company was removed, but the canopy at the front of the building retained the Northern Coachbuilders name until it was demolished in 1985. Housing now occupies the site whilst Chimney Mill, a listed building, still stands, but converted to office accommodation. Built by John Smeaton, it was a five-sailed smock mill, standing on the site of an earlier windmill. Last used in 1892, the sails were removed in the 1920s, and the distinctive cap replaced by wooden cladding in 1951. John Smeaton is best known for building the third Eddystone lighthouse in 1756. This was removed stone by stone and rebuilt on Plymouth Hoe, where it stands as a landmark and tourist attraction.

The wheel had turned full circle, with the Benfield Road works repairing, painting and occasionally building new bodies for cars and commercial vehicles. Maintenance contracts were held with Newcastle Breweries and Shell Petroleum, the work involved the repair, steam cleaning and repainting of their trucks and tankers from the local depots.

The only buses known to have entered the premises were those of HW Hunter of Seaton Delaval. This was another maintenance contract, to repaint the vehicles and prepare them for their Ministry of Transport re-certification examinations. The Hunter fleet consisted entirely of Leyland vehicles, included two double-deckers, and was known for the smart turn-out of its maroon and cream buses and coaches.

This phase in the life of the company lasted until the end of 1956, when the remaining staff moved from Benfield Road into the Smiths factory at Team Valley. Initially they were segregated into their own area of the premises, continuing their own line of business. On 19th December 1961 Northern Coachbuilders was consigned to history when the name was changed to Smiths Delivery Vehicles Ltd and became part of the Smiths Electric Vehicles Group.

What then of those who had striven to build and maintain the company? Malcolm Smith, while retaining a financial interest in the companies of the Ringtons group, devoted more of his time to the world of equine business. However, the specialist team he had recruited during and just after the war were still active men in their prime, certainly a long way away from retiring.

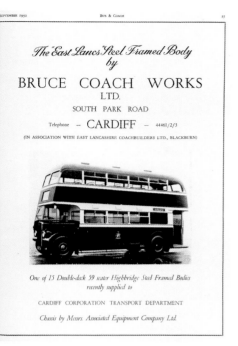

Northern Coachbuilders was not alone in coming to an abrupt and unexpected end. Brush was busy promoting its models at the 1950 Motor Show, above, yet within a matter of months had pulled out of coachbuilding completely.
(Senior Transport Archive, both)

Because their influence was so important, and because they still had years of active working life ahead of them, they went on to be key players elsewhere in the industry. Accordingly, for the benefit of those who like to trace the careers of such people, we have gathered the information together here to make it easier to follow and make no apology for any repetition this has caused.

Bramham, for instance, was only 51, having been born on New Year's Day 1900. He left NCB in May 1951 and joined East Lancashire Coachbuilders in a consultative capacity, acting as a technical representative for both East Lancashire and the associated Bruce Coachworks until late 1952. He then joined Saunders Roe on Anglesey, again as a technical representative, at the time when that company was extending its range to include more double-decker bodies. Saunders finished bus building in 1956 (later restarting in 1968) but whether Bramham stayed until 1956 has not been verified.

Horace William Heyman was still with NCB when Claremont Road closed, but was unaffected by this for, as recounted in Chapter 15, he was then in charge of Smith's Electric Vehicles and not connected with NCB. Horace William Heyman was born in Berlin in 1912 but most of his education was in this country, and he graduated from Birmingham University in 1936. He had been apprenticed to AEG in Germany, then working his way up through Electricars and Metropolitan Vickers before joining Brush when they acquired Metrovick in 1945. He had spent the war years at Metrovick on battery-electric vehicle development, following similar employment with Electricars Ltd.

He joined NCB in 1946 as manager of the Electric Vehicle Department from Brush Electrical Engineering, the parent company of Brush Coachwork. Malcolm Smith brought him into the NCB team in 1946 to support Hatton and to allow him to devote more time to bus bodywork. Heyman was knighted in 1976 for his work in attracting industry and educational opportunities to the north east. He had by then become managing director of Smiths Electric Vehicles Ltd, the company that he developed and is still in existence though now based in Washington, Co Durham with a wide range of products.

Horace Hatton came to NCB from Brush where in 1940 he was Chief Designer of Brush Coachwork, the coachbuilding side of the Brush concern and set up as a separate Limited Company, being appointed Acting General Manager in July 1940. He left to join NCB as Chief Designer in January 1944. His design work at Brush had included the huge 106-seat double-deck trams for the Mumbles Railway which introduced electric traction there in 1929, and the streamlined centre-entrance double-deck trams for Sunderland a few years later.

In addition to his double-deck bus work at NCB, he designed a completely new range of battery-electric vehicles. Hatton was unhappy with the loss of work to the Smith's Electric Vehicle company and, combined with the events caused by the BET single-deck saga, looked for other opportunities. His departure from Claremont Road in November 1947 in connection with those BEF Federation bodies problems is recorded in Chapter 12. He and John Herdman (his Chief Draughtsman, see below) left to join Barnards of Norwich, a company new to coachbuilding, in September 1947, where they assumed similar responsibilities, Hatton becoming Coachworks Manager. Barnards was soon selling a range of single-deck bodies, together with a double-deck design that owed a great deal to the former NCB 'standard' 7ft 6in wide body, as shown on page 162, but Barnards ceased coachbuilding in 1950. Hatton was appointed as production manager at East Lancashire Coachbuilders in March 1950. Later he went into a family business in Scarborough, where his sisters owned the Grand Hotel.

John Herdman joined NCB in 1942 as an apprentice, working at both Claremont Road and Cramlington. After gaining experience in all aspects of the practical work, he was asked to go into the Cramlington drawing office, which was being run by Alf Bramley. He became NCB's senior draughtsman, but departed NCB as recorded above in 1947. He left Barnards at the end of

1950, working at Churchill Constructors of Norwich from January until March 1951, and then moved to James Whitson's at West Drayton in Middlesex. He was on the coach and single-deck bus design teams of both companies. His big break came when he was taken on by Weymann's of Addlestone in Surrey in 1952. From there he was given the opportunity to go to Bus Bodies (SA) Pty in South Africa, where he rose to become Managing Director, a post he held until his retirement.

SN Churchill had been apprenticed at Harringtons, working his way up through several companies until he too arrived at Brush Coachwork Ltd, in 1943. He took the position of Chief Draughtsman, vacant following Hatton's departure for NCB. He held that position until 1946 when he moved to Charles Roberts, railway wagon and rolling stock builders, at Horbury, becoming Technical Officer of the road vehicle department. He left to join NCB in May 1949, becoming Works Manager of the company. In 1950 he departed to coachbuilder Longford's of Neath in south Wales, becoming General Manager. He remained there until 1953 when the firm closed.

During the war Richard Booth had been appointed Production Director. He left in April 1947 and so far no further details of his career have come to light.

In late 1944, the Cramlington office staff had moved back to Claremont Road, where Alf Bramley was appointed Chief Draughtsman under Hatton, who was establishing his new department. Bill Moore, the former Chief Draughtsman, went into the contracts department. Donald MacArthur and Ralph Surtees were brought in from the setting-out shop. Other names remembered from that era were Andy Nichol, John Manning, Harry Nixon, 'Tommy' Brannigan (son of operatic bass singer Owen Brannigan) and Tom Drysdale; there were others, of course. In 1946 Alf Bramley left to join Saunders Roe in Anglesey as Chief Draughtsman in their new bus building enterprise. Ralph Surtees became his replacement, but he died suddenly the following year. Herdman was by now the 'senior man', the post of Chief Draughtsman was not filled and Hatton oversaw all the work. When Hatton left to join Barnards in September 1947, he asked Herdman to join him there as his Chief Draughtsman. The void in the NCB drawing office was filled by Donald MacArthur until Bramham and his new team arrived.

Jack Graham had been a GR Haugh employee at Fenkle Street, with responsibility for repair work. He came to Claremont Road immediately prior to World War 2, then to Benfield Road in 1946, and finally Smiths at Team Valley. He left to join Associated Coachbuilders of Sunderland, before becoming manager at Picktree Coach & Engineering Co Ltd of Chester-le-Street. Former NCB draughtsman Doug Pargetter was also there. He designed the Picktree bus and coach bodies supplied to Northern General between 1948 and 1954.

There seem to have been fairly frequent movements in the Sales Manager's position. In July 1939, soon after Malcolm Smith assumed responsibility for running the Company, John Angus was appointed to that position. He had previously been Sales Manager at Massey Bros in Wigan, but before that Sales Manager at English Electric in Preston. Horace Beck, who had been with Titanine specialist paints, then took the position until he left to join Mann Egerton in 1949, as its Sales Manager.

Only thirty years separated the beginning and end of an imaginative enterprise for north east England. From modest beginnings had come great promise enhanced, it must be admitted, by the wartime orders that brought prominence to the company. This comment must not be allowed to detract from the company's achievements, because there were several other coachbuilders given the same opportunities and who failed to profit from them.

The authors estimate that approximately 860 bus and coach bodies were built by NCB, and though the number of commercial vehicle and other bodies is unknown, it certainly ran into several hundred. Add to that the battery-electric vehicles, all the special repair work and coachpainting, and it is plain that the overall output was considerable.

It seems fairly clear that NCB was one of the more successful coachbuilders of the early post-war years. From beginning as a regional concern producing 'bespoke' commercial and passenger bodywork, the company emerged from the war years in no stronger position than a number of others. Nevertheless, in a very short while it was supplying bodywork to a score of large bus operators and several independents between Scotland and the south of England.

Comparisons with other coachbuilders are not easy, because of their different aims and product range. For example, JS Robson of Blackhill, Consett in Co Durham produced more bus and coach bodies than NCB, but they were much smaller vehicles, and their main production period was between the late 1920s and mid-1930s.

Geographically, the nearest comparable firm to NCB was the old-established and reputable Charles Roe factory in Leeds, where about 1,000 single and double-deck bodies of composite construction were produced between 1946 and 1950. Roe customers, based mainly but by no means exclusively in the north of England, were steady and consistent in returning there for repeat orders over long periods of time.

Massey Bros of Wigan was a small coachbuilder with a long history, and had built bus and tram bodies for many operators in the north-west. Their post-war production amounted to almost 1,000 bodies, with a number of customers further afield than before the war. The company was probably the closest of any to the NCB capability and design at the time, but with a much longer pedigree.

The company with the greatest similarity to NCB was East Lancashire Coachbuilders of Blackburn. Bus bodies were first built there in 1938, and a number of double-deckers were supplied during the war, including the London Transport trolleybuses mentioned in Chapter 6. During the time of this survey, 689 bodies were built, including 319 sub-contracted to other small coachbuilders due to lack of space at the factory.

The company whom many people confuse with Northern Coachbuilders is Wigan-based Northern Counties Motor & Engineering Co. Established in the 1920s, NCME had developed an 'all-metal' design during the 1930s, and was allowed to produce utility bodies using this method of construction during the war. Their early post-war years saw the production of 607 bodies in the same time that NCB built 587. Not only that, but the NCME production went largely to Scotland and north-west England, whereas the NCB customer base was no larger, but covered a greater area at that time.

It cannot be denied that NCB had problems, but they were the same ones that faced all other coachbuilders at the time. Principal amongst these was the shortage and quality of material, and moreover the unions were also becoming intransigent in their attitude to wages, hours and proposed new methods of production. Add to that the fact that the whole population had just endured a long and difficult time during the war, and only the most capable were able to survive.

Nevertheless, it can be said that the aim of Northern Coachbuilders to become a national supplier was successfully achieved. Their accomplishments were entirely the result of the efforts of everyone at NCB to design, manufacture and sell products that were reasonably priced, attractive in appearance and available without undue delays. It is a measure of this success that they are still remembered with nostalgia, and that several of their vehicles have been saved from the scrap heap to be preserved as a record of the contribution that NCB made to the transport industry.

Four of the final delivery of **NCB** bodies stand outside the **Aberdeen Corporation** main bus servicing facility at **King Street** garage in 1951. The radiators were soon painted silver and then, later, chromium plated. A new general manager brought in a simplified livery in 1953 and replaced the 'universal' destination displays with separate destination and route number boxes in the whole Aberdeen bus fleet. The whole batch of ten which had been purchased for tram replacement were rebodied by **Alexanders** in 1960 and number 160, the first, has been preserved by the **Aberdeen and District Transport Trust**. *(A&DTPT Collection)*

Taking a layover in Aberdeen city centre, the driver is following the advice shown on the side of his bus. This photograph clearly shows the light grey roof, and the elaborately shaded lettering. Standing at the **Wales Street** terminus, off **Castle Street**, number 161 is working the tram replacement service for which the vehicles were purchased. The photograph was one of a series showing that adverts, introduced in 1951, need not detract from the vehicle's appearance. *(A&DTPT Collection)*

Facing page upper: **Newcastle Corporation** was the best customer for the new design taking 40 mounted on **AEC 9612A** chassis, with clutch and manual gearbox. Built between July and November 1950, this was the penultimate delivery from the **NCB** factory. *(Geoff Burrows)*

Facing page lower: One of the final batch of 'standard' **NCB** bodies, photographed before entering service in **Sheffield**. Delivered to the city in 1950 they went on to give many years service, the last not being withdrawn until 1966. *(Courtesy Sheffield Transport Study Group)*

Postscript – Barnards

We saw earlier how Horace Hatton left NCB to pursue other activities in November 1947, and with John Herdman (his Chief Draughtsman) left to join Barnards of Norwich, a company new to coachbuilding, in September 1947, where they assumed similar responsibilities, Hatton becoming Coachworks Manager. Barnards soon produced a range of single-deck bodies, together with a double-deck design that owed a great deal to the former NCB 'standard' 7ft 6in wide body shown overleaf, before ceasing coachbuilding in 1950. By good fortune Author Geoff Burrows has kept a Barnards' catalogue which shows just what Hatton and Herdman did for the company.

Opposite: Barnards' blacksmiths were artists in wrought iron – if the company had built tramcars Hatton could have had the finest dog gates in the industry. (Geoff Burrows collection)

B A R N A R D S

W. Le Neve Bower
Managing Director

H. W. Hatton,
A.M.I.MECH.E.
Coachworks Manager

MANUFACTURERS OF DOUBLE AND SINGLE DECK SERVICE BODIES, LUXURY COACHES, COMMERCIAL VEHICLES, BATTERY ELECTRIC VEHICLES AND ALL CLASSES OF TRAILERS.

In formulating this introduction it would perhaps be appropriate if I quoted " Transport World " July 8th, 1948, where describing coach building at Norwich, it is stated, " We were impressed by the great potentialities for modern body building by Barnards. Here is a large well equipped sawmill, ample floor space, with reserves of coach building necessities, with amazing stocks of timber—including the hardwoods needed, and such encouragements to self-help as a ferrous and non-ferrous foundry, well equipped machine shops and plating departments."

A manufacturing organisation with experience, production facilities, served by craftsmen and guided by highly qualified technical and administrative staffs, can be expected to produce of the best, in whatever field their activities cover. It is because of this truth that Barnards can be expected to produce, under my managership, the finest coachwork this country has known.

Barnards Ltd., established in 1826, have provided consistent evidence of high standard manufacturing ability. They have, for example, been manufacturing for over 100 years, a variety of trucks and trailers for every conceivable industrial and agricultural use, whilst they are well known as the originators and sole makers of mixed mesh galvanised wire netting. Their contribution to general and precision engineering is substantial, and they have gained a world wide reputation for wrought iron gates and fencing of all descriptions.

This brochure describes the services of our new coach building departments, and shows several examples of the various service bodies, luxury coaches, commercial vehicles, etc., which are being manufactured.

There is no job too complicated ; no job too large or small, with which we cannot deal, and I would welcome enquiries and the opportunity of placing the whole of our facilities at your disposal for the production of composite coachwork of distinction.

BARNARDS LIMITED
NORFOLK IRON WORKS, NORWICH

TELEPHONE : NORWICH 20554.   TELEGRAMS : BARNARDS, NORWICH.
MOUSEHOLD WORKS : SPROWSTON, NORWICH.   TELEPHONE : NORWICH 20554 (MOUSEHOLD EXT.).
LONDON : 110, CANNON STREET, E.C.4.   TELEPHONE : MANSION HOUSE 8597.   TELEGRAMS : BARNARDS, CANNON, LONDON.
BIRMINGHAM : 28—30, FLORENCE STREET, BIRMINGHAM 1.   TELEPHONE : MIDLAND 0269.   TELEGRAMS : BUSIBEE, BIRMINGHAM.

Catalogue No. B30

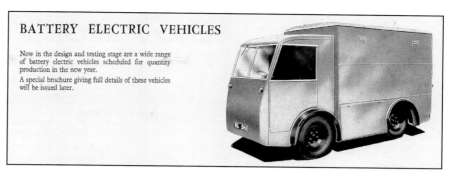

Now in the design and testing stage are a wide range of battery electric vehicles scheduled for quantity production in the new year.

A special brochure giving full details of these vehicles will be issued later.

Above: This extract from the catalogue shows that Hatton clearly intended that Barnards would be involved in electric vehicle production though this apparently did not come to fruition. *(Geoff Burrows collection)*

Barnards' single-deck coach had echoes of several designs, but, not surprisingly, none of them showed any remote affinity to the BET's Federation body. Hatton stands with John Herman in this view as they look over the drawings. *(Geoff Burrows collection)*

BARNARDS LUXURY COACH BODIES

These bodies are of the finest composite construction and are of very pleasing appearance. Six half drop windows are fitted. The interior finish is of the highest quality, hand polished walnut being used throughout. Thirty-three full luxury type seats, trimmed in moquette and hide are fitted, and every care is taken to give the maximum comfort to the passengers. Interior parcel racks and large capacity luggage boot are standard fittings.

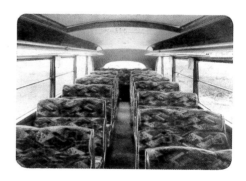

BARNARDS

DOUBLE DECKER SERVICE BODIES

Est. 1826

56 seater high bridge double decker body of composite construction. "Fastflex" Patent glazing and toughened glass throughout. Destination boxes, painting, seating and furniture to customers' specification.

A pair of hand forged wrought iron Entrance Gates and Grille, designed by Thomas Jeckyll and made by Barnards for the Bank of England. The treatment is of wrought iron work of the period of the early 18th century.

If London Transport was angry with NCB for the use of advertising without consent how, one wonders, did Aberdeen react to this gem? Even the original registration number, **BRS 559**, is still visible on this heavily retouched print based on the original (seen in context on page 97) shown at the right.
(Geoff Burrows collection)

No such ticklish problems here though as Barnards confirm that Hatton, seen at the centre in the picture, is now *their* man in this advert after the 1948 Motor Show, just months after he left Claremont Road. The wording in the advert reads –

'When Horace Hatton joined Barnards only one possible result could occur – the finest possible coachwork. Coaches built by Barnards Ltd are incomparable in roadworthiness.'
(Senior Transport Archive)

The first double-decker body built by Barnards was shown at the Commercial Motor Show at Earls Court in September 1948. It was a Guy Arab registered JC 9540 and was one of a pair for Clynogg & Trevor of North Wales (the other is shown below), in a maroon and cream livery. John Herdman was manning the Barnards' stand at the show when a rather unkempt man in overalls, flat cap and wellingtons climbed aboard. "Can I help you?" asked John. "And who might you be, son?" was the reply. Full of pride, John answered "I'm the man who designed this." "Well, son" he said with a smile, "I'm the man who ordered it!"
(Senior Transport Archive)

TRANSPORT WORLD, December 9, 1948   47

coaches built by
BARNARDS
go a long way

When Horace Hatton joined Barnards only one possible result could occur—the finest possible coachwork. Coaches built by Barnards Ltd. are incomparable in roadworthiness.

MANUFACTURERS OF DOUBLE AND SINGLE-DECK SERVICE BODIES, LUXURY COACHES, COMMERCIAL VEHICLES, BATTERY ELECTRIC VEHICLES, ALL CLASSES OF TRAILERS.

BARNARDS
COACHWORK OF *distinction*
BARNARDS LTD OF NORWICH   TEL 20554

Appendix I

Northern Coachbuilders Ltd
Bus & Coach Bodies

Year	Customer	Chassis	Reg. Nos.	Type	Qty.	Notes
1934	Newcastle Education Committee.	Commer Raider	AVK 305, BBB 310	B20F	2	Perimeter seating.
1934	Wilkinson (Sedgefield), Co Durham.	Leyland LT5A	UP 8965/6	C32F	2	
1935	Newcastle CT.	Daimler COS4	BTN 109-13	B34R	5	Metal-framed.
1935	Newcastle Education Committee.	Commer Raider	BVK 700, CTN 618	B20F	2	Perimeter seating.
1935	Chisholm (Diamond), Craghead. Co Durham.	Bedford WTL	CBB 381	B26F	I	
1936	Darlington Triumph.	Leyland TS2	HN 6676	B34R	I	Re-body.
1936	Darlington Triumph.	TSM HA39A7	BHN 903/9	C34R	2	
1936	Newcastle Education Committee	Commer PN3	DTN 596	B20F	I	Perimeter seating.
1936	Bell, Westerhope, Northumberland.	AEC Regal II	JR 5091	C32R	I	
1936	South Shields CT	Daimler COG5	CU 3569/70	B32F	2	
1937	South Shields CT.	Daimler COG5	CU 3793	B32F	I	
1937	Young, South Shields.	Leyland TS2	CU 2603/4, UW 6270	C32F	3	Original bodies rebuilt and modernised.
1937	Darlington Triumph.	TSM HA39A7	CHN 887/932/995, DHN 102	C34R	4	
1937	JJ Baker, Quarrington Hill, Co Durham.	TSM HA39A7	BUP 805	C32F	I	
1937	Newcastle CT.	Daimler COG5	EBB 187-191	H28/24R	5	Metal-framed.
1937	The Eden, West Auckland, Co Durham.	Bedford WTB	EBB 349	DP26F	I	
1937	Raisbeck, Bedlington, Northumberland	Thorny Dainty FB4/1	JR 6164	FB24F	I	
1937	Fish & Appleby, Choppington, Northumberland	Thorny Dainty FB4/1	JR 6165	FB26F	I	
1937	Foster, Otterburn, Northumberland.	Thorny Dainty FB4/1	JR 6319	FC26F	I	
1937	Wheatley, Coundon, Co Durham.	Thorny Dainty FB4/1	CPT 507	?	I	
1938	Darlington Triumph.	Leyland TS8	EHN 351/2/653	C35F	3	
1938	Newcastle CT.	Guy BTX	FVK 109	H33/27D	I	Trolleybus. Metal-framed.
1938	Tait, Knowesgate, Northumberland.	Bedford WTB	JR 8080	C26F	I	
1938	Frazer, Prudhoe, Northumberland.	Bedford WTB	GVK 414	C26F	I	
1938	Demonstrator.	Bedford WTB	HTN 133	C26F	I	Registered HTN 133 in 1939, sold to Harris, Leven, Fife.
1939	Darlington Triumph.	Leyland TS8	EHN 654-6	C35F	3	
1939	Newcastle CT.	Daimler COG5	HTN 222-239	H31/25R	18	
1939	Merthyr Tydfil CT.	Bristol K5G	HB 5875-9	H30/26R	5	
1939	Merthyr Tydfil CT.	Bristol K5G	HB 5880	L27/26R	I	
1939	Merthyr Tydfil CT.	Bristol L5G	HB 5881-3	B36R	3	
1939	Moffit, Acomb, Northumberland.	Bedford WTB	JR 9689	C26F	I	
1939	Appleby & Jordan, Choppington, Northumberland	Bedford WTB	JR 9953/4	C26F	2	
1939	Galley, Newcastle.	Bedford WTB	HTN 662-5	C26F	4	
1940	Darlington Triumph.	Leyland TS8	FHN 757/8	DP35F	2	
1941	Leigh CT.	Leyland TD7	FTB 11	L27/26R	I	Wartime utility body.
1941	Birmingham CT.	Leyland TD7	FON 628	H30/26R	I	Wartime utility body.
1941	Western SMT.	Leyland TD7	ACS 744	H30/26R	I	Wartime utility body.
1941	Sheffield CT.	Leyland TD7	HWA 276/7	H30/26R	2	Wartime utility body.
1942	Youngs', Glasgow.	Leyland TD7	XS 5493	H30/26R	I	Wartime utility body.
1942	Barton, Beeston, Nottingham.	AEC 0661	FVO 322/3	L27/28R	2	Wartime utility body.
1942	Ebor, Mansfield, Nottingham.	AEC 0661	FVO 199	H30/26R	I	Wartime utility body.
1942	Western Welsh.	AEC 0661	CKG 288/290	H30/26R	2	Wartime utility body.
1942	Western Welsh.	AEC 0661	CKG 289/291	L27/26R	2	Wartime utility body.
1943	Northern General.	AEC 661	CN 5240/1/4/7, CN 5506/7, FT 2524, UP 6821/ 7532-4, MY 2102	H30/26R	12	Utility re-body
1943	Tyneside Tramways.	Leyland TD1	TY 6970/3/7398, TY 7913	H30/26R	4	Utility re-body
1943	Tyneside Tramways.	Leyland TD3	TJ 4511	H30/26R	I	Utility re-body
1943	Cumberland MS.	Leyland TD1	CK 4172/4602, GE 2403/2499/ 7200, RM 6621/3/5/8, RU 9494, TM 3736 ,VW 8823.	L27/26R	12	Utility re-body
1943	Cumberland MS.	Leyland TD2	GW 1285, HV 2822	L27/26R	2	Utility re-body
1943	Ribble MS.	Leyland TD1	CK 4211/17/22/34/68, CK 4404	L27/26R	6	Utility re-body
1943	Wigan CT.	Leyland TD7	JP 4707	L24/24R	I	Utility re-body
1943	South Wales Transport.	Leyland TD5	CCY 993	L27/26R	I	Utility re-body
1943	Griffin, Brynmawr, Breconshire.	Leyland TD2	EV 7308	L27/26R	I	Utility re-body
1943	Leon, Finningley, Yorkshire.	Leyland LT5A	JP42	H30/25C	I	Utility re-body
1943	Kearsey, Cheltenham.	Leyland TD1	WH 3302/5/8/10	H30/26R	4	Utility re-body
1943	Kearsey, Cheltenham.	AEC 661	JO 1636, 2385	H30/26R	2	Utility re-body
1943	Venture Transport (N'castle) Ltd , Consett, Co Durham.	Maudslay SF40	BPT 789	B40F	I	Utility re-body
1944	Northern General.	AEC 661	CN 5245	H30/26R	I	Utility re-body
1944	Tynemouth & District.	AEC 661/0661	CN 5243/5508, FT 3433/4/5	H30/26R	5	Utility re-body
1944	Wakefields Motors.	AEC 661	FT 2609	H26/24R	I	Re-built top deck.
1944	Bournemouth CT.	AEC 661	TR 9454/5/6	H30/26R	3	Utility re-body.
1944	Bournemouth CT.	AEC 661	LJ 5800/1/3/4	H30/26R	4	Rebuilt bodies.
1944	Westcliff-on-Sea MS, Southend.	AEC 661	HF 7435/7	H30/26R	2	Utility re-body.
1944	Benfleet & District, Hadleigh, Essex.	AEC 661	WN 4761	H30/26R	I	Utility re-body.
1944	Canvey & District, Leigh Beck, Canvey, Essex.	AEC 661	VX 4108	H30/26R	I	Utility re-body.

Year	Customer	Chassis	Reg. Nos.	Type	Qty.	Notes
1944	West Riding Automobile Services.	Leyland TD4	HL 8611	L27/26R	1	Utility re-body.
1944	Great Yarmouth CT.	AEC 0661	EX 3691	H30/26R	1	Utility re-body.
1944	Great Yarmouth CT.	Leyland TD5	EX 5010	H30/26R	1	Utility re-body.
1944	Rawtenstall CT.	Leyland TD3	TJ 2468	H30/26R	1	Utility re-body.
1944	Darlington Triumph.	TSM HA39A7	DHN 102	B35F	1	Utility re-body.
1944	Cumberland MS.	Leyland TD7	EAO 702	L27/26R	1	Utility re-body.
1944	Wilts & Dorset MS.	Leyland TD1	UF 7382/7/90/1/9, UF 7404/12	L27/26R	7	Utility re-body.
1944	Hebble MS, Halifax.	Leyland TD4	JX 3595	L27/24R	1	Utility re-body.
1944	Swan Motor Co, Swansea.	Daimler CWA6	FNY 515	H30/26R	1	Utility re-body.
1944	Harper Bros, Heath Hayes, Staffordshire	Leyland TS3	DH 7344	H30/26R	1	Utility re-body.
1945	Stockton CT.	Leyland TD5c	CUP 252/4	H30/26R	2	Utility re-body.
1945	Grimsby CT.	AEC 661	JV 4694/5	H30/26R	2	Utility re-body.
1945	United Automobile Services.	Leyland TD2	HN 9012	H30/26R	1	Utility re-body.
1945	Rawtenstall CT.	Leyland TD3	TJ 2469	H30/26R	1	Utility re-body.
1945	Devon General.	Leyland TD4	BDV 13-16	H28/24R	4	Utility re-body.
1945	Hebble MS, Halifax.	Leyland TD4	JX 2534/6/7/3594	L27/26R	4	Utility re-body.
1945	Scout MS, Preston.	Leyland TS6	CK 4898/9	L27/26R	2	Utility re-body.
1945	Moore Bros, Kelvedon, Essex.	AEC 661	WL 9068	L27/26R	1	Utility re-body.
1945	Bournemouth CT.	AEC 661	LJ 5802/5,	H30/26R	2	Utility re-body.
1945	Sunderland District.	AEC 661	UP 6819/22/4	H30/26R	3	Utility re-body.
1945	Manchester CT.	Crossley Mancunian	EVR 350	H28/26R	1	Rebuilt body.
1945	Bolton CT.	Leyland TD4	WH 6857/9/60/1, WH 7808/9, WH 5402	H30/26R	7	Utility re-body.
1945	LPTB.	Guy Arab	GLF 680	H30/26R	1	Utility re-body.
1945	LPTB.	Guy Arab	GYE 83-93/5-7, GYL 333-44	H30/26R	26	Sub-contracted by Park Royal.
1945	Middlesbrough CT.	Leyland TD3c	XG 2327/33/4//9/41	L27/26R	5	Utility re-body.
1945	Middlesbrough CT.	Leyland TD3c	XG 2335	L27/26R	1	Relaxed utility re-body.
1945	Northern General.	AEC 661	CN 5246	H30/26R	1	Utility re-body.
1946	Bolton CT.	Leyland TD3	WH 4909/10	H30/26R	2	Relaxed utility re-body.
1946	Bolton CT.	Leyland TD3c	WH 5403/4/5501/2	H30/26R	4	Relaxed utility re-body.
1946	LPTB.	AEC 0662	ELP 238/84	DP34F	2	Bodies rebuilt to LPTB '10T10' design.
1946	LPTB.	AEC 0662	ELP 215/26/32/39	DP30F	4	Bodies refurbished and rebuilt.
1946	LPTB.	AEC 'Q'	DGX 223	B32C	1	Components manufactured, not used returned with the damaged chassis.
1946	Manchester CT.	Crossley Mancunian	AXJ 980	H28/24R	1	Rebuilt body.
1946	Sunderland District.	AEC 661	UP 6820/3/5/6/8	H30/26R	5	Relaxed utility re-body.
1946	Wilts & Dorset MS.	Leyland TD1	RU 9493	L27/26R	1	Interim utility/post war design re-body.
1946	LPTB.	Leyland LPTB	CGF 97/8, DGY 385-7/9/402/15/9/30, DLY 575/6/602	H40/30R	13	Special LPTB trolleybus design re-body.
1946	LPTB.	AEC 664T	DLY 623/6/9/33/5/41/3	H40/30R	7	Special LPTB trolleybus design re-body.
1946	Bradford CT.	AEC 661T	KY 8210/7-9, AAK 423/4	H30/26R	6	Special B'ford trolleybus design re-body.
1946	Northern General.	AEC 661	FT 2523	H30/26R	1	Re-bodied with p'type std p/w body.
1946	Bolton CT.	Leyland TD3	WH 4901/5	H30/26R	2	Re-bodied with p'type std p/w body.
1946	Bolton CT.	Leyland TD3c	WH 5503/5	H30/26R	2	Re-bodied with p'type std p/w body.
1946	Bolton CT.	Leyland TD4c	WH 6866/7813	H30/26R	2	Re-bodied with p'type std p/w body.
1946	Northern General.	AEC 661	FT 2522/5, CN5246	H30/26R	3	Re-bodied with p'type std p/w body.
1946	Northern General.	SOS REDD	HA 8002	H30/26R	1	Re-bodied with p'type std p/w body.
1946	Tyneside Tramways.	AEC 661	CN 5242	H30/26R	1	Re-bodied with p'type std p/w body.
1946	Wakefields Motors, North Shields, North'land	AEC 661	FT 2611	H30/26R	1	Re-bodied with p'type std p/w body.
1946	Holder Charlton-on-Oxmoor, Oxfordshire	Guy Arab	BUD 65	H30/26R	1	Re-bodied with p'type std p/w body.
1946	Bolton CT.	Leyland TS7c	WH 6851/2/3	H30/26R	3	Re-bodied with p'type std p/w body.
1946	Aberdeen CT.	Daimler CWD6	BRS 556/8-68	H30/26R	12	Standard post-war body.
1946	Northern General.	AEC 0661	ACN 167-176	H30/26R	10	Standard post-war body.
1946	Felix Motors, Hatfield, Yorkshire.	AEC 0661	EYG 622	H30/26R	1	Standard post-war body.
1946	Maidstone CT.	Sunbeam W	HKR 1-12	H30/26R	12	Standard post-war trolleybus body.
1947	South Shields CT.	Karrier W	CU 4716-8	H30/26R	3	Standard post-war trolleybus body.
1947	Aberdeen CT.	Daimler CVD6	BRS 569-581	H30/26R	13	Standard post-war body.
1947	Dundee CT.	Daimler CWD6	YJ 9039-58	H30/26R	20	Standard post-war body.
1947	Blackburn CT.	Guy Arab	ACB 901-12	H30/26R	12	Standard post-war body.
1947	Northern General.	Guy Arab	GPT 977-86	H30/26R	10	Standard post-war body.
1947	Severn, Dunscroft, Yorkshire.	Leyland PD1	FWW 480	H30/26R	1	Standard post-war body.
1947	Northampton CT.	Daimler CVG6	ANH 150-69	H30/26R	20	Standard post-war body.
1947	Truman, Shirebrook, Nottinghamshire.	Daimler CVD6	LNU 213-5	H30/26R	3	Standard post-war body.
1947	Hants & Sussex MS.	Leyland PD1	FCG 523-5	H30/26R	3	Standard post-war body.
1947	Yorkshire W.D.	Guy Arab	HD 7811-25	H30/26R	15	Standard post-war body.
1947	Wilson, Stainforth, Yorkshire.	Guy Arab	FYG 44	H30/26R	1	Standard post-war body.
1947	Northern General.	Guy Arab	ACN 507-516	H30/26R	10	Standard post-war body.
1947	Hants & Sussex.	Leyland PD1	FCG 526-8, FOR 837	L29/26R	4	Standard post-war body.
1947	Bradford CT.	AEC 0961	EKU 524-43	H30/26R	20	Standard post-war body.
1947	Bradford CT.	AEC 661T	KY 8206/14/20, AAK 420/1/6/7/30/1/2, AAK 434	H30/26R	11	Standard p/w re-bodied trolleybus.
1947	Green Bus, Rugeley, Staffordshire.	Guy Arab	NRE 542-3	L29/26R	2	Standard post-war body.
1947	Maidstone CT.	Daimler CVG6	JKO 638-40	H30/26R	3	Standard post-war body.
1947	Northern General.	Guy Arab	GUP 787-806	H30/26R1	20	Standard post-war body.
1947	South Shields CT.	Karrier W	CU 4873-7, 4943-7	H30/26R	10	Standard post-war trolleybus body.

Year	Customer	Chassis	Reg. Nos.	Type	Qty	Notes
1947	Sheffield CT/JOC.	AEC 0961	KWB 48-50/81-7	H30/26R	10	Standard post-war body
1948	Sheffield CT/JOC.	Crossley DD42	KWB 11, KWB 88-96	H30/26R	10	Standard post-war body
1948	Sheffield CT/JOC.	Daimler CVD6	KWB 881/66/910/1/4, KWE 29/30/1/2/38	H30/26R	10	Standard post-war body
1948	Transport Vehicles (Daimler) Ltd. (Demonstrator)	Daimler CVD6	GHP 259	H30/26R	1	Std p/w body. Sold to Northern Roadways, Glasgow.
1948	Bradford CT.	AEC 661T	KY 8200/1/5/7, AAK 429	H30/26R	5	Standard post-war rebodied trolleybus.
1948	South Western, Ceylon.	Guy Arab	IC 433-6	H30/26R	4	Standard post-war body, teak framed, with tropical heat reduction features.
1948	Yorkshire Traction.	Leyland PS1	BHE 441	B32F	1	BEF body design.
1948	Glasgow CT.	AEC 9612E	FYS 171-190	H30/26R	20	Standard post-war body.
1948	Cumberland MS.	Leyland PD1	GAO 761-780	L27/26R	20	Standard post-war body.
1948	Naylor, South Normanton, Nottingham.	Guy Arab	MNU 777	H30/26R	1	Standard post-war body.
1948	Stratford Blue Motors.	Leyland PS1	GUE 246-255	B32F	10	BEF body design.
1948	Newcastle CT.	Sunbeam S7	LTN 499-528	H39/31R	30	Standard p/w trolleybus body 30ft long
1948	Green Bus, Rugelry, Staffordshire.	Guy Arab	PRE 882	L29/26R	1	Standard post-war body.
1948	City of Oxford MS.	AEC 0961	MWL 980-4	L26/26R	5	Standard post-war body.
1948	City of Oxford MS.	AEC 9612A	MWL 985-993	L26/26R	9	Standard post-war body.
1949	Newcastle CT.	BUT 9641T	LTN 554-578	H30/26R	25	Standard post-war trolleybus body.
1949	Huddersfield JOC.	AEC 9612E	ECX 420-425	L27/26R	6	Standard post-war body.
1949	Tynemouth & District.	AEC 9612A	FT 6557-64	H30/26R	8	Standard post-war body.
1949	Glasgow CT.	Daimler CVD6	FYS 101-120	H30/26R	20	Standard post-war body.
1949	Newcastle CT.	AEC 9613E	NBB 251-280	H30/26R	30	Standard post-war body.
1949	Northern General.	Guy Arab	BCN 127-135	H30/26R	9	Standard post-war body.
1949	Northern General	Guy Arab	BCN 136	H30/26R	1	Std p/w body, metal framed upper deck.
1949	City of Oxford MS.	AEC 9612A	NFC 311, NWL 709-718	L27/26R	11	Standard post-war body.
1949	Bradford CT.	AEC 661T	KY 8213, AAK 422/5/8/33	H30/26R	5	Standard post-war rebodied trolleybus.
1949	Sheffield CT.	AEC 9621E	MWA 825-834	H30/26R	10	Standard post-war body.
1950	Newcastle CT.	Sunbeam F4	LTN 529-553	H30/26R	25	Standard post-war trolleybus body.
1950	South Shields CT.	Sunbeam F4	CU 5100-5/5279-82	H30/26R	10	Standard post-war trolleybus body.
1950	Northern General.	Guy Arab	BCN 877-887	H30/26R	11	New standard 8ft wide body.
1950	Gateshead OC.	Guy Arab	BCN 821-826	H30/26R	6	New standard 8ft wide body.
1950	Cleethorpes CT.	BUT 9611T	GFU 692-695	H28/26R	4	New standard 8ft wide trolleybus body.
1950	Newcastle CT.	AEC 9612A	NVK 311-350	H30/26R	40	New standard 8ft wide body.
1951	Aberdeen CT.	Daimler CVG6	DRS 360-369	H30/26R	10	Standard post-war body.

Notes

This list only records the passenger vehicle bodies that have been positively confirmed as built by NCB.

Because company records have not been found, the years shown are approximations of when work began on each contract.

The chassis manufacturers basic designations are shown as built; changes may have been made to them after entering service.

No Guy Arab 'Mark' numbers are shown, as the manufacturer did not use them during the period covered by this history.

For full details of the vehicles, please refer to the appropriate publications of the Omnibus Society and the PSV Circle, to whom we are indebted for much of this data.

Photographer James Riddell recorded this line-up of five rebodied Bolton Corporation Leyland Titan TD4cs in April 1945, with the torque converter tanks clearly seen on the bulkheads. The first two are 17 and 18 (WH 6859/60), and the remaining three are believed to be 32, 15 and 33 (WH 7808/6857/6861). Close examination reveals that upholstered seats are fitted, these will have been recovered from the earlier bodies. *(James Riddell)*

Appendix 2

Customer List – Buses & Coaches

Aberdeen CT.
Appleby & Jordan, Choppington, Northumberland.
Baker, JJ (G & B Motor Services), Quarrington Hill, Co Durham.
Barton Transport Ltd, Beeston, Notts.
Bell, Westerhope, Northumberland.
Benfleet & District Motor Services, Essex.
Birmingham CT.
Blackburn CT.
Bolton CT.
Bournemouth CT.
Bradford CT.
Cleethorpes CT.
Cumberland Motor Services Ltd.
Darlington Triumph Services.
Devon General Omnibus & Touring Co.
Diamond (Chisholm), Craghead, Co Durham.
Dundee CT.
Ebor, Mansfield, Notts.
Eden, West Auckland, Co Durham.
Felix, Hatfield, Yorks.
Fish & Appleby, Choppington, Northumberland.
Foster, Otterburn, Northumberland.
Galley, Newcastle.
Gateshead Omnibus Co Ltd.
Glasgow CT.

Great Yarmouth CT.
Green Bus, Rugeley, Staffs.
Griffin, Brynmawr, Breconshire.
Grimsby CT.
Hants & Sussex Motor Services Ltd, Emsworth, West Sussex.
Harper Bros, Heath Hayes, Staffs.
Hebble Motor Services Ltd, Yorks.
Hick's, Braintree, Essex.
Honour, Charlton-on-Oxmoor, Oxford.
Huddersfield JOC.
Kearsey, Cheltenham.
Leigh CT.
Leon, Finningley, Notts.
London Passenger Transport Board.
Maidstone CT.
Manchester CT.
Merthyr Tydfil CT.
Middlesbrough CT.
Moffit, Acomb, Northumberland.
Moore Bros, Kelvedon, Essex.
Naylor, E & Sons, S. Normanton, Derbyshire.
Newcastle upon Tyne Education Dept.
Newcastle upon Tyne CT.

Also built in 1945 was the first prototype post-war standard body, already seen on page 94. Here the excellent broadside view clearly illustrates the shorter rearmost window in the lower saloon, necessitated by the 26ft AEC Regent chassis on which this replacement body has been fitted. The contrast with the utility bodies for Bolton Corporation, built around the same time, could not be greater. *(James Riddell)*

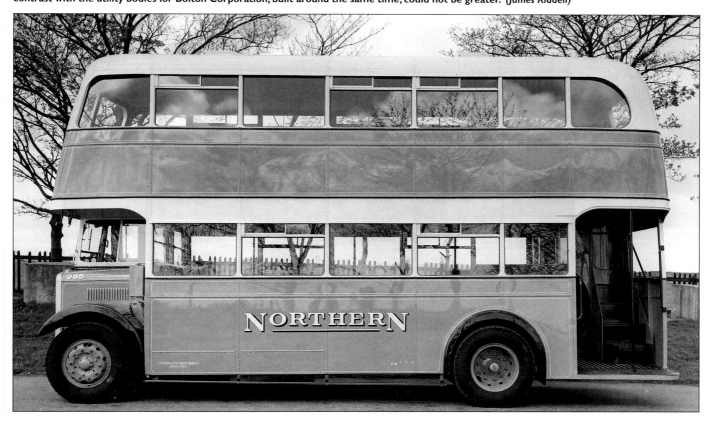

Appendix 2

Customer List – Buses & Coaches – continued

Northampton CT.
Northern General Transport Co Ltd.
Oxford (City of) Motor Services Ltd.
Premier (Harold Wilson), Stainforth, Yorks.
Raisbeck, Bedlington, Northumberland.
Rawtenstall CT.
Ribble Motor Services Ltd.
Scarlet Band, West Cornforth, Co Durham.
Scout, Preston.
Severn, Dunscroft, Yorks.
Sheffield CT & JOC.
South Shields CT.
South Wales Transport Co Ltd.
South Western Bus Co., Ceylon.
Stockton CT.
Stratford Blue Motor Services Ltd.
Sunderland District Omnibus Co Ltd.
Swan, Swansea.
Tait, Kirkwhelpington, Northumberland.
Transport Vehicles (Daimler) Ltd.
Truman, Shirebrook, Notts.
Tynemouth & District Transport Co Ltd.
Tyneside Tramways & Tramroads Co.

United Automobile Services Ltd.
Venture Transport (Newcastle) Ltd.
Wakefield's Motors Ltd. Percy Main, North Shields
West Riding Automobile Co Ltd.
Westcliff-on-Sea Motor Services Ltd.
Western SMT Co Ltd.
Western Welsh Omnibus Co Ltd.
Wheatley, Coundon, Co Durham
Wigan CT.
Wilkinson, Sedgefield, Co Durham.
Wilson (Harold), Stainforth, Yorks.
Wilts & Dorset Motor Services Ltd.
Wray, Summerbridge, Yorks.
Yorkshire Traction Co Ltd.
Yorkshire Woollen Dist. Transport Co Ltd.
Youngs', Glasgow.
Young, South Shields.

Abbreviations.
CT - Corporation (or City) Transport
JOC – Joint Omnibus Committee
Yorks. – Yorkshire

Although not the best print in this book the caption it carried relating to this Cleethorpes trolleybus spoke volumes – 'the trolleybus that ECW never built' – *ie* what Bramham might have produced at Lowestoft if ECW had ever been called to build such a vehicle. *(Bob Kell collection)*

Appendix 3

Commercial Vehicle Bodies

This list shows some of the commercial vehicle bodies built by NCB and GRHaugh. It is believed to be only a small proportion of the total output. In addition, many vehicles were sent to NCB for painting and signwriting. These, and the many bodies repaired by the company, have not been recorded.

Aynsley Iron Works. Reo lorries.
Bainbridge, Newcastle upon Tyne. Ford, Commer & Guy delivery vans.
British Ropes. Commer demonstration vehicle.
Cameron's Brewery, West Hartlepool. Thornycroft brewer's dray.
Carrick's Bakery, Gateshead. Delivery vans.
Clarkson. Reo lorries.
Collieries (various). Domestic coal tipper lorries.
Currie & Co., Newcastle upon Tyne. Foden furniture vans.
Domestos Ltd. Commer vans.
Dove, JT Karrier builders supply vehicles.
Economic League (The). Karrier van.
Hall Bros. Reo lorries.
Hoults Ltd, Newcastle upon Tyne. Leyland Cub & Lion removal vans.
Hunter's The Bakers, Gateshead, Co Durham. Morris delivery vans & Commer travelling shop.
Lambton, Hetton, Joicey Collieries Ltd. Karrier tipper lorries.
Leech, Morpeth, Northumberland. Builders lorries.
London & North Eastern Railway. Fordson local delivery dropside lorries, de-mountable road/rail furniture containers.
McPhee. Reo articulated trailers.
Minories Garages (Rootes Group Main Agents). Commer & Karrier bodies.
Muckle, Redpath. Northumberland, Thornycroft lorry.
Nobel Explosives, Glasgow. Arran freight lorry.
North Eastern Electricity Supply Co Ltd, Newcastle upon Tyne. Various support services vehicles,
North Riding (Yorks) County Council. Albion lorries.
Presco cleaners, Newcastle upon Tyne, Morris van.
Ringtons Ltd, Newcastle upon Tyne. Horse drawn tea vans, Fordson & other delivery vehicles.
Ritchie, Hetton-le-Hole, Co Durham. Thornycroft Sturdy lorry.
Robinson, Stockton-on-Tees, Albion lorry.
Silkburn Coal. Reo rigid & articulated delivery lorries.
Smiles (for miles) Transport, Blucher, Northumberland. Reo vans & lorries.
Sobel. Reo lorry.
Sparks Bakers, West Hartlepool. Commer delivery vans.
Taylor's Foundry, South Shields. Leyland flatbed lorry.
Topham, Masham, North Yorkshire. Bedford horsebox.
United Automobile Co Ltd, Darlington. Bedford parcel vans.
Wilson Electric Vehicles Ltd. Van body.
Wimpey (George) & Co Ltd. Commer tipper lorries.
Wright. Reo lorries.

By the mid-1930s manufacturers of small vans (eg Austin, Morris, Ford, Commer/Hillman and so on) were producing complete vehicles on car-type chassis. Specialist coachbuilders such as NCB were only required for bespoke vehicles. One such was for Presco Dry Cleaners who needed a tall body for racks of full-length clothing. This little Morris is a l0cwt series II model with 12 hp engine and hydraulic brakes, but only a 3-speed gearbox. The engine was offset to the nearside so that the driver could sit well forward and leave space for the load. (Bob Kell collection)

Appendix 4a

Battery-electric Vehicle Customers

Co-op Dairies
Co-op Travelling Shops
Thomas & Evans (Corona)
Bakers
Butchers
Dairies
Grocers
Greengrocers

Exports to :-
Belgium
Canada
Denmark
Eire
New Zealand

Appendix 4b

Model Range

Three-quarter Ton
One Ton
One and a quarter Ton
One and a half Ton
Two Ton
Walker-NCB Four Ton Refuse Wagon

All except the Walker-NCB refuse wagon were available as Dairy Floats, Enclosed Vans, Open Vans, Travelling Shops, Open Trucks or chassis only. Special bodywork for customers was built on request. Painting and signwriting were to customers requirements.

Talks on Trade Terms — NO. 9

By MALCOLM SMITH, Managing Director, Northern Coachbuilders Ltd.

"battery electrics"

The power unit of the Battery Electric Vehicle may well give thirty years of useful service. To match this superb mechanical efficiency the coachbuilder must work to very high standards. He must design bodywork for strength and durability —and yet obtain such pleasing lines and finish as will not outdate the vehicle early in its life. This we have achieved at N.B.C. We are producing the N.C.B. Battery Electric Vehicle which is a quality production throughout. Chassis and body are by N.C.B., electrical equipment by B.T.H. and batteries by Exide. The vehicle is produced in a range of specialist body types for the milk, laundry, bakery and general delivery trades and in all respects bears the stamp of N.C.B. Craftsmanship.

 NORTHERN COACHBUILDERS LTD.
Claremont Road, Newcastle upon Tyne, 2.

Builders of fine Coachwork and Makers of the N.C.B. Electric Vehicle.

Appendix 5

NCB Vehicles in Preservation

It is remarkable that at least five examples of Northern Coachbuilders bodywork have survived into the 21st Century. Of even more interest is the fact that two of the examples above demonstrate the classic post-war design, whereas the other two clearly show the effects of the Bramham era. Top left, Northampton Daimler 154 (ANH 154) was delivered to the Corporation in June 1947, while top right Maidstone 72 (HKR 11), a Sunbeam W, entered service in April that year. These days the Maidstone vehicle may be found operating at the Trolleybus Museum at Sandtoft. Lower left, GFU 692, A BUT trolleybus, was delivered to Cleethorpes Corporation as their No. 59 in July 1950 with Bramham inspired features. At present it is undergoing restoration at Sandtoft. Finally Newcastle 341 (NVK 341), an AEC Regent, entered service in October 1950 and is seen here alongside former South Shields No. 1 (ECU 201E) a Bristol RE with Eastern Coachworks body which demonstrates the design progression at that company which had been started by Bramham. The fifth preserved example is illustrated on the rear cover. (John A Senior, David Cole (2) and Clarence Carter).

MISCELLANY

What has the 1930s Dinky Toys 'futuristic' model bus to do with Northern Coachbuilders? Just enough to warrant inclusion!

Holland Coachcraft was formed in Govan, Glasgow in 1931 by William Hawthorn Holland. His ideas from the 1920s were far ahead of the then commercial vehicle industry and were to move the driving position forward alongside the engine and transfer the load-carrying area forward between the axles. Holland, therefore, had to alter chassis to these principles before constructing bodywork. He closed the Govan factory in 1933 and licensed his plans to coachbuilders throughout the UK. At the November 1933 Commercial Motor Show he created a sensation with a streamlined Commer 2ton van. Demand increased and in 1935 Meccano Ltd adopted the Art Deco style van as a 'coach' for the Dinky Toys range.

Problems with contracted coachbuilders led Holland (as Holland Coachcraft Ltd) to open a factory at the new Team Valley Trading Estate in Gateshead. This was the first Government-supported industrial estate in England to encourage alternative employment in areas of declining heavy industry. Plans in 1936 foresaw the build of 700 commercial bodies per year but contracts with large organisations failed and in 1940 with no Ministry of Supply permits to purchase materials in wartime, the factory closed. It was reopened by Sigmund Pumps but converted to the manufacture of Bren Guns in 1941. In 1950 the factory was taken over for the manufacture of Smiths NCB electric vehicles as their manufacturing base.

Much of Holland's direct or licensed production were the spectacular Art Deco vans of the 1930s as shown by the Castlebank Laundry's Albion van. Castlebank, of Anniesland, Glasgow operated at least eight of these vans (in yellow colours!) on house-to-house collection and delivery of laundry. The legend on the front of the van says it all. "Mother, Here Comes the Castlebank Man".

As far as is known, no coaches or buses were built although plans for them existed. The Dinky Toy is thus speculation, but may have been taken from Holland drawings. A double-deck coach would surely have been spectacular.

MISCELLANY

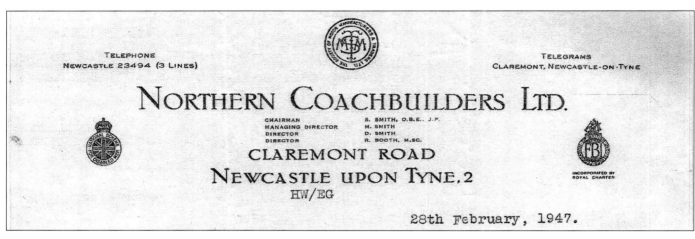

Two letterheads showing, upper, Sam Smith as Director in the pre-war version. Note the references to Reo Motors and GR Haugh. By 1947 in the lower example his son Malcolm is now Managing Director following the death of his elder brother Sam Smith (Jnr) in a flying accident. Richard Booth is Production Director. *(Authors' collections)*

Finally – a splendid view of two of the Triumph fleet in their original 1938 condition, photographed by Roy Marshall.
(Bob Kell collection)

Darlington Triumph purchased a series of seven TSM model HA39A7 chassis in 1936/7. The operator maintained a coachbuilding shop in Darlington, but called upon **NCB** to supplement their own production which the authors consider was restricted to just one vehicle BHN 948. This photograph is believed to show the first of the 'NCB six', probably BHN 903 or BHN 909, and has been professionally coloured to represent the Triumph livery. Another TSM chassis was also given a similar NCB 'Triumph' body (BUP 805) with the addition of a roof luggage rack for JJ Baker of Quarrington Hill, Durham. *(Geoff Lumb collection)*

This remarkable survivor, below, is still with its original owners E & N Ritchie in Hetton-le-Hole, County Durham. A 1939 Thornycroft with **NCB** body and cab, it is one of several vehicles retained for preservation and restoration by Colin Ritchie. Over the years it had a variety of uses, including delivery of bagged coal. At one time it carried a cattle transport body, but after making a 14-hour journey from Durham to Reading at a top speed of 24mph, it reverted to more local work! *(Bob Kell)*

One of the longest-lived wartime NCB bodies was that fitted to this 1936 Grimsby Corporation AEC Regent, number 55, JV 4695. It was photographed opposite the Victoria Street depot working hard in May 1961 when a number of buses with wartime bodies were still in service in the fleet. The view of the upper deck rear window shows it to be one of the 1945 bodies with the later 'square' emergency window lights. Sixteen years was a good life for the 'stop-gap' utility body. (*Bob Kell*)

NCB also produced many components and assemblies for WW2 aircraft as mentioned in the text. The Fairey Aviation Swordfish served with the Royal Air Force and Fleet Air Arm during WW2. Affectionately known as the 'Stringbag', more than 4,000 were built, used mainly as bombers and torpedo launchers, as seen in the picture below. Despite having a top speed of little more than today's High Speed Trains, they were capable of performing actions that were difficult for the enemy to counter. A flight of Swordfish sneaked up on the German battleship Bismark in 1941 and damaged it so severely that it was unable to escape from the big guns of the Royal Navy ships chasing it. The pride of the German navy was sunk in the ensuing battle.
(Tony Higgett, courtesy Wikipeadia)

No photographs of the NCB version of the Park Royal bodied Guy Arabs built for London Transport are known to exist. This picture, though, show what they would have looked like in their post-war livery. One of the original Park Royal versions has been fully restored, and was photographed at Cobham Museum in 2009. *(Graham Smith)*

NCB were authorised by the Ministry of Supply to build new bodies on new 'unfrozen' chassis and this is the first. It is their first wartime lowbridge body built on the assembled chassis of a Leyland Titan TD7 for Leigh Corporation and completed in November 1941. It was only NCB's second lowbridge body after Merthyr's HB 5880. The bus is shown when it was with Moore's 'Viceroy' fleet in Saffron Walden, Essex. Later acquired for preservation it is currently in the St Helens Transport Museum. *(Geoff Burrows Collection)*

London Transport trolleybus 97 (CGF 97) was one of a number severely damaged in June 1944 at Bexleyheath depot during the Blitz on London. Originally a short wheelbase type, London Transport rebuilt it with a full length chassis frame, before sending it to NCB for a new body. Reclassified D2C and renumbered 97C, it was returned to Bexleyheath depot. It is seen here in later days in Welling on route 696 to Dartford. *(Michael Dryhurst)*

In 1946 six NCB trolleybus bodies were built for Bradford to an interim design, illustrating many of the features that were to be used for the standard post-war version. Known by Bradford enthusiasts as 'Mk I', 622 (AAK 424) was photographed at the Thornton terminus. The AEC chassis had previously carried English Electric bodies when new in 1935. *(Jim Copland, courtesy Geoff Lumb)*

One of the first post-war standard **NCB** bodies was built for this 1932 Northern General AEC Regent. In this 1951 photograph it is standing in Park Lane, Sunderland, still used on 'main line' services. *(Allan Condie)*

It seems fitting that one of the first post-war trolleybuses built by **NCB** has been preserved. This Maidstone Sunbeam W is cared for at the Sandtoft Museum. *(Alan Millar)*

The first **NCB** trolleybus for South Shields is seen here in the Hudson Street cutting about to pass underneath the **LNER** railway at Tyne Dock station. The photographer was standing on the bridge that led to the house where the grandparents of one of the authors lived. The trolleybus is on the counter-clockwise town circular service from Tyne Dock to Pier Head via Westoe. Number 246 was in use from 1947 to the end of 1962. *(Geoff Burrows Collection)*

Dundee's 20-strong batch of NCB double-deckers was long lived although they had no doubt received attention by the Transport Department coachbuilders. In January 1968, after almost 21 years of service, No. 160 (YJ 9047) and another on the right, are no longer in all-day service, but wait outside Maryfield depot with other early post-war stock to take up peak hour duties. *(Bob Kell)*

Once their early problems had been solved, the Blackburn Guy Arabs with NCB bodies had long lives, and three survived into preservation. Their original green Blackburn livery had been simplified over the years, and this September 1983 view of No.74 (ACB 902) in preservation shows it in a later version. The bus survived in the St Helens Transport Museum. *(Bob Kell)*

The 1946/7 batch of bodies for Aberdeen had a longer life than the later examples. They were not withdrawn until 1961-4, and apparently needed less rebuilding than bodies from other manufacturers in the fleet. Note the 'utility' driver's windscreen which was all that was available to NCB at the time, and compare it with those on the 1951 versions. Number 71 (BRS 579) a Daimler CWD6 stands alongside one of Aberdeen's ten AEC 'RTs' whose Weymann four-bay body with deep windscreen illustrates the lower driving position of this chassis. Both buses display the new manager's destination display. *(A&DTPT Collection)*

The design of this 1958 Smith's milk float is virtually the same as the original version built by **NCB** from 1946. This one can be seen at the museum of the Birmingham & Midland Motor Omnibus Trust, Wythall, near Birmingham. *(Birmingham & Midland Motor Omnibus Trust)*

Facing page upper: The AEC Regent III chassis usually graced the products of most coachbuilders, and the batch of 20 for Bradford in 1947/8 was particularly handsome in mid-blue and cream with lining out and grey roof (although the photographer has coloured the roof blue). The bus is undergoing its tilt-test at Cramlington prior to receiving its certificate of fitness. No NCB bus ever failed this test. *(Ringtons)*

Northampton bought the first 20 Daimler **CVG6s** built for the home market in 1947. The straightforward Northampton red and white livery showed off the well-balanced design of the **NCB** double-deck body to good effect. Withdrawal of the batch began in the 1960s, but No.154 (ANH 154) was saved from destruction when it was converted into a driver training vehicle in 1964, and later for publicity use. It was bought in 1990 by a group of enthusiasts and painstakingly restored to its former glory. Apart from the addition flashing indicators, 154 looks as it did in original condition when appearing at the Netley (Southampton) Rally in July 1995. *(Geoff Burrows)*

Facing page lower: In June 1961 Bradford celebrated 50 years of trolleybus operation, and two trolleybuses were selected to represent the earlier liveries. Pride of place was taken by 603 (KY 8206), a 1934 AEC 661T chassis with 1947 NCB body, in this portrayal of the first tramway-derived livery, seen during a special tour of the system. The second vehicle is Bradford 687 (CAK 687) with the original Weymann body in 1939 livery. The third trolleybus was representative of the contemporary fleet and livery with an East Lancashire-bodied chassis. *(Bob Kell)*

Three Daimler CVG6 buses were built for Maidstone Corporation in 1947. Though having slightly earlier chassis numbers, they left the NCB factory after the first Northampton models. Number 74 (JKO 638) is shown in the final version of the Maidstone 'toffee brown' livery, complete with 'home-made' ventilator in the front dome. *(Geoff Burrows collection)*

The South Shields trolleybus system was expanded rapidly after World War II, and 23 NCB-bodied vehicles were bought to operate it. In 1947/8 ten Karrier F4s entered service, and No. 255 (CU 4877) was one of them. Though obviously in run-down condition when pictured in the Market in 1960, the structure was clearly still sound. Some of the bomb-damaged buildings surrounding the Market had just been demolished in this view, to make way for new shops. *(Geoff Burrows collection)*

The Stratford Blue Leyland Tigers all found ready buyers when withdrawn and sold. Most went to Welsh operators but GUE 248 headed for the far north east of Scotland. Was it the most northerly NCB body? Dunnets Motors of Keiss, north of Wick, appear to have retained the Stratford blue but repainted the wings white. One of this batch, GUE 247 (Stratford No. 41) still survives in preservation at the Birmingham and Midland Motor Omnibus Trust at Wythall. (R Marshall/Omnibus Society)

The only Yorkshire Traction NCB-PS1, BHE 441 of April 1949, was pensioned off in 1960 but then fitted out, believed to be with a rear chair-lift, to provide transport for the Barnsley Handicapped Services Committee. Yorkshire Traction still owned it, however, and it served a further six years in this role. (R Marshall/Omnibus Society)

This view is a rare colour picture of one of the final batch of AECs supplied to Sheffield. It was photographed on a rather misty January day in 1963 at the Pond Street bus station. (Paul Fox)

The early post-war Glasgow fleet used a great variety of coachbuilders to body its new AEC, Albion and Daimler chassis, and NCB built the bodies on 20 AECs in 1948 and 20 Daimlers in 1949. Shown at Anniesland Cross in May 1961 on its way from the city to Drumchapel, A89 (FYS 189), an AEC Regent III, is painted in the original livery, though the 'via' blind box has been taken out of use and painted over. The vehicle was allocated to Knightswood garage, and had another four years of work in Glasgow. *(Iain MacGregor)*

Cumberland Motor Services was supplied with 20 lowbridge NCB bodies on Leyland PD1 chassis in 1948/9. This picture shows 228 (GAO 766) in later life after a heavy body overhaul revealed by the new panels and glazing. It was renumbered 315 in 1961, and is seen here in Millom. *(Geoff Lumb)*

Since the restoration of this Newcastle Sunbeam trolleybus was completed at Beamish, it has visited several other museums. The photograph shows it operating at The Black Country Living Museum in 2008. *(Mark Lyons)*

This AEC Regent III with NCB lowbridge bodywork was seen entering Manchester Street bus station, Huddersfield, in October 1961. Number 221 (ECX 421) was one of six purchased by the Huddersfield Joint Omnibus Committee in 1949. *(Geoff Lumb)*

Grimsby-Cleethorpes number 162, an NCB-bodied BUT, was originally delivered to the latter undertaking as its number 62 in 1951. The combined undertaking was established in 1957 and shared a joint route between the two towns. Number 62 then became 162 as seen at the boundary between the two towns. *(Jim Copland, courtesy Geoff Lumb)*

Aberdeen Corporation NCB-bodied Daimler CWD6 bus No. 69 of 1947 is shown in Castle Street by the Mercat Cross of 1608. This area was used as a waiting area for standby buses and it appears to have come from Aberdeen Royal Infirmary as a duplicate. The photograph was taken late (between 1956 and 1959) in its career with ACT which came to an end in 1961. Note the redesigned destination box layout, the simplified livery and the reinforced bulkhead pillars. Number 69 went on to become a travelling showroom and later a control room with the Aberdeen & District Motor Club and was only broken up in the 1990s. *(A&DTPT Collection)*

Index

NCB people see personnel
Illustrations shown thus **2**

In June 1982 an outing in this preserved bus included a visit to the former Claremont Road coachworks in Spital Tongues. Posed beside the 'NCB' lettered canopy of the works where it was built, No. 341 (NVK 341) is a tribute to the design, and the craftsmanship of the builders. The bodywork has only needed minor attention despite re-entering service with the Tyne & Wear PTE in public service in 1977/8. Soon after this photograph was taken, the empty factory was demolished, but the bus remains in excellent condition at the time of publication of this book. The Ringtons Tea advertisement is most appropriate. *(Bob Kell)*